T0146779

No Longer Lonely, Balboa Press, U.S.A. 2012
Also by Ray Buteau:

Those In Power

WITHOUT INCLUSIVITY AND EQUITY, THE CATHOLIC INSTITUTION WILL QUICKLY DECLINE

Ray Buteau

BALBOA
PRESS
A DIVISION OF HAY HOUSE

Balboa Press books may be ordered through booksellers or by contacting:

Balboa Press
A Division of Hay House
1663 Liberty Drive
Bloomington, IN 47403
www.balboapress.com
1 (877) 407-4847

Because of the dynamic nature of the Internet, any web addresses or
links contained in this book may have changed since publication and may
no longer be valid. The views expressed in this work are solely those
of the author and do not necessarily reflect the views of the publisher,
and the publisher hereby disclaims any responsibility for them.

The author of this book does not dispense medical advice or
prescribe the use of any technique as a form of treatment for physical,
emotional, or medical problems without the advice of a physician,
either directly or indirectly. The intent of the author is only to offer
information of a general nature to help you in your quest for emotional
and spiritual well-being. In the event you use any of the information
in this book for yourself, which is your constitutional right, the author
and the publisher assume no responsibility for your actions.

Any people depicted in stock imagery provided by Thinkstock are
models, and such images are being used for illustrative purposes only.
Certain stock imagery © Thinkstock.

Print information available on the last page.

ISBN: 978-1-5043-2900-2 (sc)
ISBN: 978-1-5043-2901-9 (e)

Library of Congress Control Number: 2015903517

Balboa Press rev. date: 04/21/2015

"The LORD has sworn
and will not change his mind:
"You are a priest forever,
in the order of Melchizedek."
– Psalm 110:4 (New International Version)

The first priest mentioned in the Bible is not from the Tribe of Levi. In fact, the first priest is described before Levi is even born. In Genesis 14, we are introduced to Melchizedek, who is described as "Priest of God Most High."

Aside from being identified in Psalm 110 and then extensively reflected upon in the Letter to the Hebrews, Melchizedek remains an elusive figure in the Scriptures. Even so, today's priests are ordained to "the order of Melchizedek," and Melchizedek's appearance in Genesis forms the basis of some of our theology of the priesthood.

"No one will be able to stand against you all the
days of your life. As I was with Moses, so I will be
with you; I will never leave you nor forsake you."
– Joshua 1:5

THOSE IN POWER

A former priest and a parishioner share their journeys through abusive relationships.

To my sister Carole

Acknowledgements

I want to acknowledge all the beautiful people who have been a part of my spiritual journey and thus, have played an integral part in the creation of this book:

- Those with whom reconciliation may not be possible but to whom I am grateful for the life lessons I have received from having known you.
- Those I have considered personal mentors and strong supporters, especially my sister, Carole.
- Darren: From September, 2006, until May, 2008, Darren worked with me in dividing the draft of my fourth manuscript into two separate manuscripts. For his insight, I will always be grateful.
- Lisa McGifford, who, in 2002, worked as a counsellor and speaker on domestic abuse. With her permission, I have used her workshop material.
- Rick Johnson of Final Copy Editorial Services, primary editor.

- Vic Hooper for his pyramid illustration. >stationv.com<
- Heather Sandilands primary proof-reader.

Thank you, and Namaste!

Contents

Preface

Wednesday, March 13, 2013, had me riveted to saltandlighttv.org and the papal elections. Then at 1:05 p.m. CST, white smoke came out of the famous Sistine Chapel chimney. I quickly phoned my sister, Carole, and blurted: "Turn your television on! A pope has been elected and white smoke is coming out of the chimney."

"Let me finish what I was doing and I'll call you right back," she said, knowing that, as with most of her calls from me, her life had to be put on hold. A minute later, after getting settled in front of CNN, she returned the call.

"I'm really happy to be watching this with you Carole," I said as we continued our small talk about the crowd in the pouring rain in Rome and the various on-air speculations while we waited for the balcony scene to unfold.

Then the doors opened and the Dean Cardinal came out with the medieval introduction, "Habemus Papam"— "We have a pope"—and then gave the name: Cardinal Jorge Mario Bergoglio!

Along with most people in the square below the balcony, my sister and I said in unison: "Who?" And then, when he gave the pope's name again, along with the crowd, we repeated, "Who?"

Finally, it was reported that he was the cardinal from Argentina and we were even more surprised since, according to the media, he hadn't been mentioned during the election as one of the favorites.

As we watched them unfold via the modern media, the events that followed were well recorded for history. Later, I was sharing the news with a young, also gay former priest, who was also in a period of transition. He made an insightful comment about the new pope. He said, "Let's watch him surprise us."

As many warmly welcome the new pontiff and anticipate seeing him do his own thing, I can't help feeling this is not going to end as many hope.

When Pope Benedict resigned, it was reported that a bolt of lightning had struck the Vatican … which was apparently photographed. It was quickly noted that lightning does strike the Vatican from time to time, and I thought to myself, *Ya, about as often as a pope resigns.*

Some were quick, again, thanks to modern media, to report that it must have been a sign that this new one will be the last pope, as predicted in the prophecy of Saint Malachi.

An online search of "The last pope" or "Saint Malachi Prophecies" suggests about 112 popes will reign before the end of the world … some fascinating reading.

On March 19, 2013, the Feast of St. Joseph, the patron of the Catholic Church, and the date of the inauguration of Pope Francis I, I found myself again watching live events unfold in Rome. It was a sunny 14 degrees Celsius there while outside my apartment in Winnipeg it was 3:30 a.m. and minus 19 degrees.

The new pope was wearing simple liturgical vestments and celebrating outside with a million people in attendance. As I watched, I thought about a comment the president of Argentina previously had made to this same man while he was Cardinal in Argentina and busy at the time fighting against gay rights, which, by the way, are legal in that country. The president referred to then Cardinal Jorge Mario Bergoglio as being from a medieval era. I agree.

St. Francis of Assisi, an Italian in the 12th century whose name the new pope had chosen, influenced history at a time when the Catholic Institution had significant religious and political influence. Today it faces an era of secularization and human evolution into inclusivity and tolerance of individual human rights.

Near the end of his life, Pope John XXIII said, "It is not that the Gospel has changed; it is that we have begun to understand it better ... The moment has come to discern the signs of the times, to seize the opportunity, and to look far ahead."

From those words forward fifty years to today, we find the Catholic Institution asking itself if it has ever adopted Pope John's mentality. How open is it to the modern world, and to what level does it adapt the Gospel, or "understand it better" within the context of the people and culture of our time?

The Catholic Institution, which had built and formed the Western World, seems more and more to be losing its control and power to shape society. It appears weary, and it looks as if the future may be determined by non-Catholic Christians and non-religious, spiritual forces.

Many of us have been brought up morally, with a sense of justice, social conscience, and a belief in a higher power. But, being in a religion of guilt, self-righteousness and judgments, we fail to see how spiritual we already are. Many are longing for the recreation of meaningful rituals that would engage more deeply a "language" of the heart, imagination and passion. Women and gay priests are uniquely able to contribute to this recreation, but both are being kept in their place and will not be able to contribute within the structure and limitations of the Roman Catholic Institution.

Not all men have lost touch with their deeper feminine selves. In fact, a large segment of the clergy is definitely in touch with their deeper feminine selves. The Catholic Institution will continue to decline until it includes female perspectives.

Gay priests are not being allowed to express, acknowledge, accept, nor celebrate these qualities because the Catholic hierarchy is in denial that gay priests have such gifts to offer the Catholic Church. The Catholic hierarchy remains in denial, labelling all gay priests as potential paedophiles in order to avoid the entire topic of homosexuality, and their acceptance of women in ministry. The issue will not go away, even if some among the clergy and parishioners do move on.

The church, like secular society, is in the midst of change. Since New Testament times, there has been a struggle between Gospel values and those of the world. We have to come to terms with a shift from religious authority to spiritual experience. We are now living in a culture of experience.

Many of us lived an experience in the Roman Catholic Institution that we couldn't find words to articulate until society gave a language for the experience of abuse. Abuse was seen as doing something that would inspire fear, and control as a choice that was aggressive or subtle. Power is the ability to enforce control. Empowerment is the ability to do something for oneself.

Future conversations with the Catholic hierarchy will become increasingly difficult because of the rise of evangelization, New Age spiritualties, and apparent cultural, ethnic, political and religious differences that require a relationship of respect in order to meaningfully converse.

FORWARD

Since childhood, I had a spiritual hunger for answers to many beliefs and doctrines that I questioned and found difficult to believe. Instead of being offered answers, I was made to feel that I was just being difficult, contradictory, and somehow unfaithful. I had no difficulty believing in a God, but it was everything that was being said about God that I had difficulty with. I was told that I had to believe all the doctrines for the sake of my soul.

I thought that words such as faith, religion and spirituality were terms for one and the same reality. I had faith in God, and my religion was Christian, though I would say Catholic. I thought of spirituality as prayers, devotions, and worship. In doing these rituals, I believed myself to be a spiritual person.

The form of spirituality that I was brought up with was expressed in going to church, receiving the sacraments, doing devotions, such as reciting prayers to saints, and going to special services in honour of saints and Christ.

At the time, spirituality had nothing to do with me as a unique person in a unique holistic relationship with God, others, and creation.

As a Catholic, I had been influenced and directed into various forms of spirituality through the works of a number of Catholic writers: St. Francis, St. Theresa, St. Augustine, St. John of the Cross, St. Bernard, St. Benedict, St. Ignatius, to name a few.

These men and women wrote at a particular time in history in which the Catholic Church had ultimate control and power, and encouraged a culture that saw virtue and sainthood in ultimate obedience. The language was one of submission, guilt, obedience, self-denial, and shaming.

Today, as I reflect on what I was taught, I see that being a Catholic, believing that I belonged to the One True Church, and growing up in a very religious home made me feel as if my connection with God was different from that of my friends, which made me feel isolated from them, at times confused, and at times on edge and full of self-doubt. I began to deny belief in certain things without my family and teachers being aware of it because I believed I could not question my beliefs. If I questioned the "True Faith" and no longer believed in what I was being taught, what would be left? What would happen to my relationship with God? What would happen to my soul if I were to die?

But the self-righteousness of many Christians had always bothered me, especially when it came to judging the salvation of others who were not Christians, such as a child born in another part of the world into a different culture, a different religion, a different value system, and with different morals. The parents of that child loved God (or their deity). They were kind individuals who respected and cared for others, and prayed daily to their deity.

Many Bible-verse-quoting Christians said those non-Christians would not be saved. I have never been able to comprehend that kind of thinking, nor have I ever been able to accept that merely being baptized assured a person of his or her salvation.

Introduction

It's difficult for some Catholics, practicing or not, to say anything negative about the Catholic Church because many of us were taught from a very young age that the Catholic Church, unlike the Protestant Church, was instituted by Christ himself, and therefore by the will of God. The Catholic Church was referred to as "Mother Church" so to say anything with the slightest tone of inquiry, would be to question the will of God. Hence, many of us accepted everything as fact or, at least, as a mystery. For many Catholics, the institution remains a strong spiritual community in which they live healthy, fulfilled lives.

Having lived in a cycle of abuse, both as a child and as a priest, my experience within the Catholic Institution was difficult. For most of my life, I couldn't share my experiences because I didn't have a language with which to articulate them, not to myself, nor to those who considered themselves my friends.

Being accepted into the seminary seemed a natural fit. I had learned to be obedient to others' expectations, which predisposed me to being abused. In the seminary, I was isolated from the worries and temptations of the world and constantly reminded that, as seminarians, we had been chosen by God. I learned how to survive by being a liar to myself and to everyone else.

As I studied the language of abuse, I became aware that I had also been in a cycle of abuse throughout my priesthood but was unable to recognize it as abuse while I was in it.

Since I relied on my parents for financial support, my mother kept me on a guilt trip and knew how to push my buttons. I always used to speak of myself as having had a happy childhood, but after reading *The Drama of the Gifted Child,* by Alice Miller, I was made aware that I was in denial of what my childhood had really been.

Those who knew me as a priest will wonder how I'm able to say such a thing—that my entire priesthood was lived in abuse—because I was surrounded by loving and caring people, both laity and clergy. I was given every opportunity for education, retreats, and clergy support. I had comfortable living accommodations, along with clerical staff and ladies groups that offered to help me maintain my residences. So where was the abuse?

What had I been feeling and experiencing that finally led me to believe abuse was present? In January, 1991, I was asked to attend addiction groups to begin to relate to words such as helplessness, powerlessness, impulsiveness, manipulation, perfectionism, control, obsessiveness, and co-dependency, I began to write about my experiences. At the time, I was cynical, sarcastic, angry, and disillusioned. It came through in my writing.

In doing research about the church, I read *Unknown Gods* by Reginald Bibby, and *The Dysfunctional Church* by Michael Crosby. Those books helped me articulate the experiences I had had and was having.

In 1995, I was introduced to Diarmuid O'Murchu's book *Reclaiming Spirituality*, which gave me a language to help me articulate my spiritual experience. He spoke of the power and control of the Catholic Institution as being in the hands of the hierarchy, which makes up as he wrote, less than one percent of the church, with the remainder being the faithful.

I adopted this reference but I speak of the one percent as being *all* those who wear pointed hats in church. They are the only ones with the power and control.

It is my view that the remainders of the hierarchy, the ordained priests, are a subculture separate from the one percent, and also separate from the faithful and the religious brothers and nuns who make up the remaining ninety-nine percent.

- In 2002, I attended a workshop for service providers in Winnipeg on domestic abuse. It dealt with the theoretical background to abuse. At that workshop, I became aware of a language that enabled me to understand my entire spiritual journey; a language that defined the following terms:
- "abuse" – doing something that would inspire fear
- "control" – a choice that is aggressive or subtle
- "power" – the ability to enforce control
- "empowerment" – the ability to do something for oneself

Recognizing Oneself in an Abusive Relationship

- direct abuse is physical abuse
- subtle abuse is the one that both Danielle and I experienced in our relationships

In this pyramid model, Diarmuid O'Murchu in his book *Reclaiming Spirituality* 1997, speaks of the less than 1% and the 99%. I have separated the 1% and the 99% to insert a subculture which is not included in either the 1% or the 99% and which I refer to as a clerical subculture.

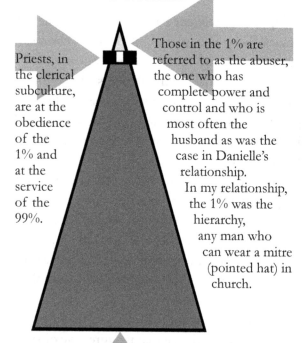

Priests, in the clerical subculture, are at the obedience of the 1% and at the service of the 99%.

Those in the 1% are referred to as the abuser, the one who has complete power and control and who is most often the husband as was the case in Danielle's relationship.
In my relationship, the 1% was the hierarchy, any man who can wear a mitre (pointed hat) in church.

The 99% are referred to as the victims.
In Danielle's family these would be their children.
In my relationship with the 1% these are the parishioners (the faithful, the laity).

4

An abusive relationship consists of one person relentlessly pursuing a position of power and control relative to another person until an imbalance of power results. Control is accomplished through intimidation and the exploitation of vulnerability, creating for the victim a chronic state of fear and anxiety. The means used may be aggressive or seemingly passive in nature. Considering this, I see my relationship with my bishop as having been abusive, not healthy.

Those who likely relate most to the insights that my spiritual journey has unraveled, and to the language of abuse I use to articulate my experiences, will be priests and the religious who have been forced into addiction programs, as well as priests and religious persons who are gay; anyone aware that they are being abused and victimized; those in minority groups who don't fit within the religious system; those who are trying to move on in their spiritual lives; and, finally, those who do not practice their Catholic faith, yet say they will die as Catholics.

PART 1

Recognizing Yourself In an Abusive Relationship

Enough!

*H*earing the term "the addicted church" always made me feel uncomfortable because it paints everyone in the church with the same brush. I was more comfortable referring to the addicted hierarchy, the one percent who suffer an addiction to power and control while priests and the ninety-nine percent enable them to remain in their addiction.

The signs of an addiction are often obvious to others but not to the addicted. Most of us know someone with an addiction. If we approach someone with our concern about their drinking, overeating, codependency, gambling, or sexual addiction, they will often insist they don't have a problem. They'll say that we are the only ones who have a problem with whatever they are doing.

This scenario would be the same if we were to approach someone within the one percent and, not fearing excommunication, express to them our concern about their abusive addiction to power and control.

Shortly after arriving at my first parish as an assistant pastor, I felt like I was back home with my mother. I was not happy. I felt trapped and wanted to run away. I had to justify everything, live up to another's expectations, and endure ultimatums and constant criticism. I was isolated, on edge, humiliated, submissive, and childish.

Every few years after that I displayed signs of withdrawal, depression, and aggressive behavior. My body tried in vain to tell me I was in an unhealthy situation. I tried to escape, but I felt trapped on a treadmill of trying to live up to an impossible ideal, stuck in religiosity, clericalism, and guilt. Like an abused housewife, I always went back for more.

I often saw myself in the young couples I met in the parishes who were also caught between expectations. I enjoyed their independent spirit and rebellious outlook. I found them refreshing and wished I could serve them without strings attached, but I could not.

Hence, because of the church's expectations, a lot of those young couples did not get involved, preferring to take a passive role and be aloof within the church.

Many priests can relate to the pain of having no one to speak to about their feelings of isolation, humiliation, helplessness, fear, and vulnerability. Many of us have seen the impact of that on others, and how the situation affected our own thinking. Many of us have been silenced.

When I finally saw that those who abuse do not change, I said, "Enough!"

Danielle

*E*arly one August morning in 2012, I opened my e-mails. One read:

Congratulations on your book, and thanks for adding your e-mail to the press release. While you were in the Interlake area, you performed our marriage about thirty years ago, and ten years ago, I also lost my title as "Mrs." I'm living in Winnipeg now and am hoping to meet with you. I'd be grateful to hear from you.

Danielle

I was intrigued. I contacted Danielle shortly afterward, and we set a date, time, and place to meet. The day quickly arrived, and after politely acknowledging that neither of us looked anything like we had back then, we enjoyed a long chat that covered many things beyond our mutual delight in meeting and how we moved on after our respective "survivals."

It wasn't long before I realized that our conversations were probably the best way to illustrate just how similar my life as an abused person in the priesthood was to that of an abused housewife.

Danielle admitted having longed for a time when she would be able to share her experiences with someone she had known during the time of her abuse.

We agreed to meet at least a few more times, but to focus each meeting on a different aspect of our experience of abuse. It would be an additional bout of catharsis for both of us, but we wanted it to be a structured learning experience as well as just a friendly sharing.

So we agreed we would focus each get-together on a different aspect of abuse and talk about it from our respective perspectives. Our next meeting would be a luncheon, and the topic would be isolation, whether physical, emotional, or social.

We were also going to try for better coffee.

Isolation

$\mathcal{D}$anielle and I had agreed to meet at the Paddlewheel Restaurant in downtown Winnipeg. It was a favorite place of mine to meet friends for lunch, with good food and an environment that was conducive to relaxed chatting. I arrived a tad early and laid claim to a secluded table for two against the far wall, away from the buffet area and most of the other guests. During the week, most of them tended to be business people, doctors, and lawyers from the immediate area with its jungle of office buildings and clinics. They were in a hurry to eat and run, so they generally took up the tables nearest the buffet.

I returned to the entrance area to wait for Danielle. She was right on time.

"Hi, Danielle," I said as she approached from the nearby elevator. "Good to see you again."

"Hi, Ray," she replied with a wide smile. "Same here. Do you think we would have recognized each other after thirty years if not for that last meeting and the e-mails?"

I laughed and said, "Probably not."

"That hat you're wearing today would not have helped," she added, "but it looks good on you."

"Thank you," I replied as we headed for different areas of the buffet to make our choices.

"A word of advice," I said before she got too far away. "When piling the salad plate, just remember you will be charged by the weight."

Back at our secluded table, we settled into our lunch. I asked Danielle if she was happy with her life—if she had adequately come to terms with everything. It had been years since she got out of the abusive relationship with her husband, Doug, just as it had been a few years since I had gained my freedom from abuse.

"Yes," she said, followed by a short hesitation before adding, "thank God! Otherwise I wouldn't have been strong enough to communicate with you, let alone actually meet with you."

"I know what you mean. That's exactly how I feel about writing my second book. I couldn't have done it back then."

She put her salad fork down, took an envelope from her bag, and passed it to me.

"What have we here?" I asked as I began to open it, but she said nothing. "Oh my …" I said as I recognized the contents. "Your wedding-day program. And there's my name as the officiating pastor. This is pretty awesome!"

"I thought you would find it interesting," she said.

"Yes, indeed," I agreed as I looked through the document from another world, my eyes finally settling on the notorious Scripture passage that many couples still include in their marriage program.

"You too," I said after silently reading it through.

"What do you mean?" Danielle asked.

"Many couples that I performed marriages for used this same passage, and I believe that if both, not one or the other, but if both had reflected on it each year on their anniversary, as I always suggested at the time, perhaps more marriages could have been saved."

"I know I'm walking right into something here, Ray, but what passage, exactly?" she asked.

"It comes from Corinthians 1, chapter 13, verses 4 through 8. In many Christian Scripture versions, including yours, it starts with 'Love is patient, love is kind.' It's here in your program."

As I finished reading it aloud to Danielle, I could see she was fighting back tears. She composed herself and said she was fine. "I'm just realizing how true all of that was … is," she corrected, "as well as your advice about reflecting upon it, and how regrettable it is that most couples never think about it at all after the wedding."

I smiled as reassuringly as I could and tried to lighten things up a bit. "So, Danielle, we're a couple of minutes into this and … well, do you think we're going to be able to talk about all there is to talk about on the subject without causing a scene in this place?"

She laughed a bit and quickly went on. "Really, Ray, it's actually you I'm most worried about."

"Oh, don't be," I said. "This oversensitive fag will do his best to keep it together."

We both laughed again and went on with our meals.

We had agreed to focus our time together on sharing our experiences with isolation, and we would come prepared with written material if necessary so that we could stay on topic. We also wanted to understand where we had each come to in our lives as survivors. After munching down awhile, I reopened the conversation.

"What was it like for you living on the homestead in the Interlake area, Danielle, after your marriage?"

She held up a finger to signal she had a mouthful of food. "Excuse me," she said finally. "This is great salad, isn't it? Now, to answer your question: As you know, I am originally from Winnipeg, but my husband's entire family was living in the Interlake where I was working. Previous generations were buried in the local church cemetery." She paused and I waited.

"In some ways," she continued, "I was very fortunate. The in-laws were great, and I felt very close to his mother and sisters. But as the months passed and I got to know them all better, I began to see the family dynamics at work."

I nodded my understanding as I continued with my lunch, and Danielle went on.

"At times, a tension showed between husbands and wives, but the women never said anything to me about their relationships. One day Doug and I walked right into the middle of his parents arguing but they quickly ended it when we appeared. What I found odd at the time was that he never said a word about it to me afterwards."

She paused for another bite and collected her thoughts again. "As the months went by, the way we spoke to each other changed. Doug stopped asking me when he wanted me to do something and instead just started telling me what to do … and then sometimes he wouldn't even bother to thank me for things I did. And when we got together with family, there was laughter, small talk, and a lot of drinking, though that was never an issue for us.

"When something needed to be decided," she went on, "Doug would make the decision without discussing it with me, and if I asked him about it, he would simply say he didn't think he was supposed to confide in me. At first, I just found that a bit odd but then it began to really bother me. Because Doug never wanted to talk about anything, we didn't … I confided in my mother.

"I had never seen that side of him before we were married," she added. "I think we had been on our best behavior during the marriage preparation classes, which we only went to for a few weeks before the wedding. With wedding invitations out, hall bookings made, and dresses on the sewing machine, it seemed like everything was all set and that it would all be just great going into the future. When we met we were madly in love. We seemed to agree on everything and we both wanted to settle down, but settling down out in the country can mean something different for each person. In our case, all eyes were on me … expectantly awaiting the news that I was pregnant. And there was another expectation I hadn't anticipated. I was to be a stay-at-home mom. My duties were about to change. Previous women in the family had set the trend and I was expected to fall in line with what I had married into."

At that point, Danielle stopped. I could see she felt quite emotional about all that had happened, even though she had been in the healing process for a long time. I kept silent and let her compose herself.

"Doug was never physically cruel to me," she began again. "He didn't have a drinking problem; he was involved in many community activities; and he didn't complain about going to church. He didn't complain about the in-laws or his work in farming. Actually, he didn't say anything about anything … I know, Ray, that you know where this is going and that is exactly why I wanted to speak with you, someone who can see the bigger picture and, from what I read in your book, I knew you would be able to relate to what I'm saying. I needed someone to understand what I went through. And somehow, though you weren't involved, just knowing you were in the same town at the same time for part of it … and actually living something similar … well, it closes the gap between us and makes this sharing so much easier."

"Yes, Danielle, I feel very similar. It's reassuring in a way … and I do see where this is going … in the same direction as what I went through. I understand why you wanted to speak with me. You and I started in isolation. We were both surrounded by people who loved us but we felt that we couldn't speak with any of them."

"That's right … and that's why I felt I needed to share my story with you. I, too, am 'No Longer Lonely,' as you put it in your book. I'm sure that sharing our experiences will help you to validate your relationship with the church."

"That's my hope, Danielle … and I have a ways to go with that. Let me try to give you an idea of where I was at as a newly ordained priest. Of course, it all began way before working in the Interlake, and it's heady, but you'll understand where I'm coming from.

"In the seminary," I began, "I lived in a very protective environment for several years. And then, with a Roman collar around my neck, I was ready for parish ministry. As a newly ordained priest, I was thriving on hierarchical, patriarchal clericalism, without even realizing it. That clericalism was maintained through control over lay involvement, rituals and teachings. Clericalism, through power and control, is essential for hierarchical authority and represents the practice of power and control in the clerical subculture. It is maintained through brainwashing, clerical power, and the demand for obedience.

"When I became a priest, I knew that I was not entering into a relationship of equal power with the bishop, just as I would not be entering into an equal power relationship with any employer.

But, in the priesthood I was always reminded by the bishop that I was co-equal, a co-worker, and that we needed each other. But the reality is that priests are employees of an institution that is also a corporation, and the bottom line relationship is one of power and control … so the one percent will find ways to exploit power differences in order to create fear in their priest employees, and thereby continue to create and maintain positions of power and control for themselves.

"For both of us, Danielle, I think what we saw as abusive was a gradual process that, at most times, was very subtle, but at other times, usually in public for me, was very direct. Do you understand?"

"Yaaa, I think so," she replied cautiously. "I understand most of that, but I'm having difficulty with your one percent and what you call a 'subculture.' Could you explain that some more?"

"Sure Danielle," I said. "Picture a triangle with one percent at the top point separated from the remaining ninety-nine percent ... and between those two sections is a separate little sliver. The one percent represents any man in the church who can wear a pointed hat, such as a bishop, a cardinal, or the pope. These are the men whom I refer to as being addicted to power and control—the one percent.

"Priests make up the subculture in the rectangle, that little sliver, and are under complete obedience to the one percent as enablers and are also at the service of the ninety-nine percent, who are the faithful. The parishioners and religious nuns are in this group as well. You and I both understand what it is like to live in a relationship with someone who is addicted to power and control ... It's isolating on purpose, because isolating someone is a very effective way to control them.

"You know, Ray, what struck me most way back in those ... those 'uncomfortable' years, was realizing how much my sense of isolation played on my situation. Did you have that same experience?"

"Yes, for sure ... and for me the sense that I was different as a priest and separate from the community added to my sense of isolation. The one percent says that priests constitute its right hand in ministry, but most priests are not that naive. The one percent has an unwillingness to engage in self-disclosure, which makes it difficult to cultivate relationships. After a while, you just don't know who you can trust or talk to, which, as you might guess, adds to the isolation."

"I often felt that living in the Interlake, in a small community," Danielle added. "If I were to say something about what was going on at home it would get out and the entire family would hear about it, and then what would I do? I think other women feel the same way, and so we all just remain on the same level."

"In my last parish," I said, "I once received a six-page letter from an anonymous parishioner saying that I was not in the parish only for them, but that they were there for me also, and I should let them into my life. I do believe that the sender was sincere and wanted to be of support to me. The only problem was that there were many aspects of my life that I felt I could not share with them."

Danielle nodded her understanding. "I always felt that our priests were somehow at a distance and that you couldn't really get to know them, not that I wanted to … sorry about that," she said with a grin, and then asked, "May I ask what you did with that letter?"

"I shared it with the pastor of the parish, and rather than be of support and speak up for me, he felt that it would be in my best interests to simply remove me from the parish. I was floored! I liked many of the parishioners, and on my last day with them I simply said that I could not live up to their expectations of me. I felt caught between a rock and a hard place. As my shrink put it, I could make a good first impression but never risked continuing the rapport, which only continued to make me feel alone and isolated. I would start a relationship with great intensity and end it abruptly. And, of course, I always felt that being gay isolated me even more."

"Weren't you close to some of the families?" Danielle asked. "I had heard that there were some families that you visited more regularly."

"Well," I replied. "A few couples became my close friends but most knew me only superficially … not intimately. As their parish priest, I felt we had a lot to talk about but, on a personal level, I felt stifled. I wanted to make friends but felt that I could not be totally open with them for professional reasons, and for fear of being judged and rejected by them. Over the years, friendships with parishioners were difficult to maintain. Although I knew I would always be welcomed by them and that they would be happy to see me, I found it difficult to withhold who and what I really am. The fear of disclosure and rejection was always there."

"Tell me about it!" Danielle replied sarcastically.

We sat quietly for a few minutes, eating, drinking and mulling over all that had been said to that point. I felt very comfortable and sensed that she did as well. We enjoyed just being silent for a while … nurturing our connection as kindred souls, until Danielle finally ended a long silence.

"As the years went by," she said, "it felt as though Doug was screening my contacts with others, and then one day my suspicions increased tenfold. I walked into a room when he was on the phone. He immediately hung up, saying to someone, 'Sorry, she's busy … talk to you later.' I asked him if the call was for me and he just said someone would be calling me back but they hadn't said why they were calling. I later found out that the 'someone' was my mother! I didn't confront him about it because I wanted to see if others had been getting the same response from him when they called me."

"And were they?" I asked.

"Yes, I started to hear friends say they had called but I was out, or busy, and they were not told anything else, and Doug would not tell me that I had received a call. I found it odd ... and unsettling, to say the least ..." She paused before adding, "I began to feel as if I was living in his house, not our house."

We sipped our coffee and went silent for another short time. I quite enjoyed those centering breaks as much as I did the conversation. They provided time to process and think about how best to move forward with our "exploration."

I decided to read a piece I had written for my next book to get her reaction.

"At clergy study days and retreats, priests were often reminded that we were co-workers with our bishop, and brother priests to each other. If the relationship with the bishop was to be considered fraternal, then some of the following qualities of a healthy adult relationship should have existed as well: mutual respect, affection, listening, an ability to think of the other person first, humor, communication, maturity, authenticity, forgiveness, and honesty. A healthy relationship exists when there is some kind of balance and equality. There are shared goals and the freedom to grow as an individual, and to offer compassion, consideration, care and challenge."

Danielle responded with eyes wide. "Ray! All of those 'qualities,' as you call them, should also have applied to me in my relationship!"

"Of course," I replied, and continued. *"Isolation is used to control priests' access to the media, other minority groups, and political involvement, which all also entrench a feeling of vulnerability."*

"That's what I felt …," Danielle jumped in, " … *vulnerable*, that's the word!"

"And the greater the isolation," I added, "the more vulnerable to fear and intimidation we will feel when facing a threat alone."

"Yes, exactly!" Danielle said in a loud voice, her hands outstretched in a kind of "ah haaa" gesture, which caught the attention of other diners at the Paddlewheel.

"Whenever I was called in to see the bishop," I went on, ignoring the curious onlookers. "I was entering *his* building, *his* office, surrounded by *his* staff, and I was alone. I was also being controlled by my perception of him. Priests often got talks about the importance of feeling a fraternal collegiality. That fraternity was also supposed to include the bishop, who always needed to remind us that he was just one of us … But, boy! Don't cross his path or this 'brother' would show his true colors … red being the dominate one!"

"May I quote you on that?" Danielle said with a chuckle.

"Sure, go ahead," I said.

"I have one word for it," she added.

"Which is?" I asked.

"Amen!"

We laughed for a few minutes at the tragedy of it all and our obvious connection as survivors to the essence of what we had each experienced.

"Danielle," I said after we had composed ourselves. "We are only just beginning … and there's so much more to share. It's almost overwhelming."

"No kidding!" she replied, and immediately continued. "At the time, I never realized how much my entire world revolved around Doug, his needs, his requests, and his schedule."

"Being away from your family, friends and even your culture," I said, "you didn't have anyone else as a reference point … talk about isolation!"

"He had me believing that my lot in life after our marriage was to be a mother of however many children he wanted. I emotionally and willingly stopped my body at three kids … and didn't tell him. He thought there was something wrong with me and told me go to a doctor. But Doug didn't want to be with me when I spoke to the doctor about such a personal thing so the doctor told me I was fine and just didn't seem to want to have more children. I told my husband the doctor had said I was fine, and left it at that … but he would often remind me of what a great place the community was for raising a family and, actually, he was right."

With that, Danielle took a breath, sipped some more coffee, and added, "Gradually, I became aware of something. Doug never asked me how I felt about having children, or about living in that community, or if I was happy. He assumed that simply being by his side and doing his bidding I would be happy. It was the same assumption I am sure he made about all the other women in his world."

"Isolation slowly blinds us to the fact that there's an outside world. I can see that was happening to you." I said. "For me, life revolved around my bishop in a similar way. He was usually willing to listen to me, even though his mind had already been made up. I knew I was expected to be obedient to his needs ... But, in reality, the submission to someone who is arrogant and self-righteous becomes humiliating, not humbling; abusive, not virtuous; and demeaning, not fulfilling, don't you think?"

"Yes, for sure, Ray, and it's amazing how your words are so right on with what I experienced and felt."

"It's taken me a long time to piece it all together, Danielle. I have stood before a bishop and had to listen to him proclaim all the authority that he had in giving me my next assignment, and the obedience that was required of me. Sometimes, I was consulted, but usually I was merely told when and where I was being sent."

Danielle nodded in understanding and empathy as I shuffled through my papers to find a particular reflection I had written down days before and wanted to read to her.

"Listen to this, Danielle ... Because of isolation, I never got any contradictory information. When made to believe that what I was taught came from God Himself, and that my bishop was the spokesperson for him, I was made to think I didn't have need of anyone else's opinion. I was dependent on my bishop and felt degraded by my dependence on him. As an abused priest, I viewed myself as not worth the effort of even leaving. The brainwashing worked in the past, but today we are becoming better educated and we are becoming aware of the dynamics of abuse in every aspect of our lives, and we are saying enough is enough!"

"Once again, Amen to that ... I can relate," she said emphatically. "I'm sure that had we lived in Winnipeg, I would have had the support I needed much sooner to have said to him, 'Enough! Enough!' But I had the children to raise and my home to maintain ... without his help. Everything in the home was mine, including painting the place, and telling Doug that if he didn't fix something I would have to get someone in to do it, and in that small community it probably have been someone related to him, would have hit him in his pride. He would never have allowed that."

She paused and I waited for her to continue.

"He was very much a man of another era," she added. "Thank God he didn't have a drinking problem. He did have a quick temper but it was over quickly. Doug made his point and I got the message." She paused again and dabbed her watery eyes with her napkin.

"You okay?" I asked.

"I'm great," she said, taking a deep breath. "Thanks ..."

We both chuckled and sipped our coffee in silence for a few minutes, and then she continued once again.

"I couldn't have left him while the children were growing up. Doug was a good provider and a good father in many ways. But he was no longer my lover and had never been my soul mate ... that emotional distance was very painful. There was no one in the community who could have helped me, and I think he knew I was firmly held in his world."

"Yes, I can certainly relate to that," I offered. "It was little wonder both of us had a sense of not fitting in. During the worst of it, I displayed what now seems like a mixture of mature and immature behavior, and I had a feeling that no one else was like me, especially being gay and a priest. All of that heightened my feeling of isolation … of not really being accepted, and afraid of anyone that I perceived to be a bully, including the bishop. I remember a bishop saying that we should not keep ourselves in isolation from one another because our distancing could lead to all sorts of addictions. But if the one who is calling us to togetherness is himself your abuser, and acting from within his own addiction to power and control, you eventually fall into all sorts of addictions as well … in order to survive in the abusive relationship and environment. If you can't beat 'em, you join 'em!"

"This may sound strange," Danielle added, "but I often felt humiliated, although Doug would never have realized it."

"That's how I often felt," I agreed, "and then felt immature for feeling that way."

"Oh, Ray, this is so good … it's so validating to be able to share all these thoughts and feelings … really cathartic."

Humiliation, Fear and Intimidation

❦

*J*ust a couple of weeks later, again seated comfortably at the Paddlewheel with our meals before us, Danielle and I almost instantly got into the next topic on our agenda—humiliation and intimidation at the hands of our abusers.

The most difficult thing for me to accept," Danielle began after our brief preliminaries, "was that my life as a person did not seem to be important. Many women would have envied my situation—good kids, a faithful husband, supportive in-laws, and a stable community. What more could anyone want, right?"

"Nothing at all," I said sarcastically. "I talked about this in *No Longer Lonely* ... how I had lived a very privileged life."

"But when I met Doug, I was a teacher and looking forward to advancements in teaching and a career. I had no idea that when we got married and had children that he would expect me to leave all that and be a stay-at-home mom. If I said anything, or even implied that I missed teaching, I wouldn't be listened to at all, only reminded of how fortunate I was to be able to stay home with the children. I always hoped that at some point I would be able to talk about my career, but as time went on, it seemed that it was over. I had had such hopes, but the message I was getting was that I was only a housewife and that was how I was to see myself. I felt I had lost my spirit somehow, even my sexuality. We had had a great sexual relationship until the family routine set in. Thank God I had wonderful kids."

She paused briefly and I jumped in. "Thank God I had some great parishioners and priest friends, but being gay was such a heavy secret it isolated me from being more open and intimate than I might have been otherwise. Priests were reminded of the sinfulness of homosexuality in letters from the bishop ... probably still are. In fact, homosexuals have been the scapegoats for the one percent throughout history. During feudal times, gays were burned. And what is really tragic is that they were often murdered by the same homophobic abusers who considered themselves peers. Yet, the one percent seems to be increasingly concerned about the role of homosexuality in the priesthood, despite the fact there is a disproportionately high number of gay men in the priesthood."

I was surprised how quickly into the conversation I felt the emotion rising inside me, and a lump forming in my throat, but I forged ahead, anxious to make my point.

"And although I'm sure you know this already, most gay priests do not abuse children."

"This is a difficult topic for you, isn't it Ray," Danielle said.

"It's beyond difficult," I choked. "It's painful … because … well, I got out but I know so many priests who still live in that world of hypocrisy. The gay community sees the attitude of the one percent on this as trying to make gay priests the scapegoats for decades of criminal abuse. If you could count all those who are homosexually oriented, the number would be staggering. Many saints and even popes were gay orientated."

I paused for a bit while Danielle continued eating, waiting for me to continue.

"It's unfortunate that Henri Nouwen, the author of *Reaching Out* (the three movements of the spiritual life) could not 'come out' while he lived. But he knew what the consequence would have been for him—he would have been silenced and rejected, and what a tragedy and a loss that would have been!"

"I too felt like I was 'abnormal' or something in the eyes of others," Danielle continued, "because all the women I knew seemed to accept their family roles … there were no women I could talk to about how they felt as women and as wives. I certainly never heard anyone talk the way I was thinking."

"That's exactly how I felt as a gay priest … I had my 'secret' but no one to talk to."

"Even amongst the women that I knew there were husbands with drinking problems and who were very rude to them in public, yet none of those women shared with any of the others ... at least not that I ever heard about. There would have been groups and family and friends to share with in larger communities, but not in a community in which so many were related."

"You're right about that, Danielle, in working situations, victims of emotional and psychological abuse can take their cases to arbitration, and even to court, but that action would be as unthinkable for a priest as it was for you in a small community. At the same time, many priests are subjected to this type of abuse, being treated like children and not as unionized adults."

"You know, Ray, I didn't even see my situation as that serious at the time, but as time went on I began to realize Doug had all the say and all the control over everything that went on. It was only when I began to realize I was just a part of all the things he controlled that I wondered who, or what I was really living with. Today, I'm able to label it 'emotional abuse,' although I couldn't see it as that in the beginning."

"For my part, my relationship with the bishop was not amiable at all, and I didn't have close contact with him other than being called in to face some issue or other. For the Roman Catholic Institution to work, when priests are ordained they have to swear allegiance to their bishop and his successors, regardless of how dysfunctional, uncompassionate, or self-seeking some of those men might be. Once ordained, we became 'one of the boys' ... part of an elite, male, celibate society with its own expectations and fringe benefits. In that respect, as you see, my relationship with my abuser was quite different from yours, but we were both under someone else who called the shots."

"I see what you're saying, Ray."

"We had yearly clergy study days and retreats at which we were reminded of our responsibilities to the one percent, and of the sacredness of our priesthood."

"The more I believed my lot in life and my relationship with Doug, the more I believed I wouldn't hear anything different from anyone else. I remember going to see my parents and meeting young couples who talked about how they shared house duties, prepared meals together, and made special times for themselves as a couple. I had at one time believed we were going to have that in our relationship."

"Danielle, on a few occasions, I stood before a bishop who accused me of something for which I was not at fault. He would take the word of an individual, or group that had made an accusation against me and I was guilty by the fact that I was perceived to be causing waves. I had to stand in front of him unable to defend myself, and not even be given the benefit of a doubt. I was made to feel that there was something wrong with me, that I was being disobedient and upsetting everyone concerned. I was subjected to this kind of humiliation on various occasions during my ministry."

"How strange it is to hear that," Danielle added, "because, as you say it, I can recall times when I would say something and then was made to feel I was wrong for even thinking it. But I didn't make anything of it at the time. I think I began to doubt what I thought and so just went along with what was expected, no longer questioning anything."

"The term is unpleasant to accept, but we become 'tamed adults'," I said.

"Not a pleasant thought," Danielle agreed. "As time went on, I began to realize I was totally dependent on Doug, not only financially, but also for all decisions. Wow! And since we no longer had an intimate relationship and Doug wasn't showing me any special attention, I began to feel degraded by my total dependence on him. I see now that teaching would have offered me some financial independence and personal fulfillment ... and less power and control from him, and less humiliation."

"The way we are treated as adults is such a personal issue for me, especially as a gay man. As a priest, I often felt so degraded and humiliated by the ongoing struggle on the part of the one percent to ensure that their priests were not dominated by homosexuals, and that their candidates were 'healthy' in every possible way. I felt like an outcast, part of a minority group within the priesthood ..."

I paused for a few seconds, and then added, "It occurs to me, Danielle, that we both experienced abuse in a very subtle way, unknown to others ... even our own abusers. Our abuse was not direct; we weren't being physically hurt, although the emotional pain was real and, for me, resulted in health issues. But we felt we were being degraded and by our total dependence, we were humiliated ... which was terrible."

"Yes," she said slowly, processing what I had said before going on herself. "After a few years, with the children in school, sports, and religion classes, I began to see myself as not worth the effort that it would take to leave him. I was truly humiliated, diminished, and that's for sure."

"Danielle, despite all the external signs of parish renewal programs engaging in outreach, many people really don't want things to change and they fear that new people might upset the organization's balance of power. It's probably the same with an abusive marriage partnership … but I know that in the Catholic Institution, the one percent has a deep vested interest in maintaining things as they are."

"Like Doug … He sure didn't want things to be different from the way they had been with his father … and his father before him."

"As terrible as our experiences were, Danielle, I thing we have to remember that we both survived because God was with us each step of the way, and continues to be, otherwise these reflections of ours would become overwhelming for us."

"I think I agree with you Ray, though I'm not as sure of it as you are." She paused for a moment and then said, "I just know I got a lot of strength out of the fact we both can still laugh."

"Amen Danielle! Amen! And maybe this is a good time to take a break. Would you like a refill?"

"Yes, please," she replied as I picked up our coffee cups and headed back to buffet area.

As I approached our table with the coffee refills, Danielle looked up and smiled broadly, but only for a second.

"Is everything okay," I said as I put our coffees down on the table.

"Oh, yes ... nothing serious ... I was just wondering if anyone here might think you and I have something going on."

I laughed a bit, sat down, and said, "Well, if they do, it's me they're wondering about because they see me here every month with different women, which probably is confusing some of the gay men with their 'gaydar'."

With that, we both had a good laugh. I had long since explained to Danielle that 'gaydar' is like a sixth sense that gay people have that tells them with fairly good accuracy if another person is also gay.

We settled back in, slowly sipping our coffees and then decided to move forward and tackle the whole topic of fear and intimidation.

"I have a little phrase that has helped me keep focused through all this Danielle ... It is fear that makes the difference between bad behavior and abusive behavior."

"Yes, that makes perfect sense to me," she replied. "I think it's what sustained the power imbalance between my husband and me ... and which kept me feeling so vulnerable. When we met," she went on, "I thought that I had met a man that had gone beyond the male expectations of his cultural community. He seemed so open minded, not sexist, interested in my views and desires. He seemed sensitive and caring, what happened to all that?"

"I don't know, but I had similar views upon entering a relationship with the church ... that it would be sensitive and caring toward me, even though I knew it was sexist ... and I would soon find out, homophobic as well. The one percent has an idealized image of itself as 'Mother Church'—a compassionate, nurturing, and caring institution with values of faith, hope and charity. But it doesn't acknowledge its own shadow or dark side; it's addiction to power and control toward its victimized groups within the ninety-nine percent, such as women, homosexuals, sexually active youths, unwed couples, and irregular church attenders, all of whom continue to feel like outsiders. It wasn't long before I began questioning the image of a compassionate 'Mother Church'."

"As time went on and we had children," Danielle added, "Doug began correcting the views of our children. I tried to speak with him about the way he was speaking to them, but the look he gave me took me back. The strong, negative, defensive energy coming from him, I'm sorry to say, frightened me. He had never frightened me before. I could feel his strength as he put me back in my place as an obedient wife and mother. If it wasn't for the children around distracting me, I think I would have lost it."

"What did you do Danielle?"

"The same thing you talk about in your book ... I cried alone ... And then later he'd say, 'Do you think I'm being too hard on the kids?' A sign of vulnerability perhaps, but before I had a chance to say anything Doug would quickly add, 'They'll understand it's for their own good.' And later, I thought to myself that he probably meant that for me, too."

"Like your husband," I said, "the one percent becomes defensive, refusing to admit to what really is happening. They say, 'trust us, give us the benefit of a doubt,' but their policy of hushing things up is consistent with their secretive, authoritarian way of handling things. They wear tinted glasses so they are unable to see themselves as abusers of power and control. They only want to protect their reputation, their idealized image of themselves, and to preserve their power structure, just as your husband was protective of his image of a strong head of the home ... and everyone in it."

"Yes, exactly! He looked at me as though I was confronting him, as though I had no right to say anything that would question him."

"It's horrible, Danielle, when you realize the relationship you're in is one in which the other party is addicted to having complete power and control over you."

Danielle sipped more of her coffee and wiped a tear from her eye as I looked for something I had written on this very point.

"Ahhh, here it is," I said as I located the page I was looking for. "*Members of the one percent will feel as if they are being accused and condemned unjustly. They won't appreciate being compared to an abusive partner. They go out of their way to be perceived as compassionate shepherds, with open-door reception for their priests ... but make an appointment first! They say they want their priests to be happy, content and fulfilled, but they are unable to deliver because they lack the compassion needed to be sincere. Compassion is impossible when the shadow side is not even acknowledged. That is why it was easy for my bishop to sit in front of me, give me the assurance that he was good at what he had to do, and then say to me that I was dismissed ... no compassion, just a ritual hug, and his 'best wishes'.*"

"I have to admit," Danielle said, "when I was a child, I was an obedient, quiet girl that never questioned anything … I respected and loved my parents. Life was simple and innocent for me."

"Yes, isn't it too bad that being used to being a 'good girl' can make a person susceptible to being bullied?" I asked rhetorically. "For my part, when I was at home, I found myself going quiet, becoming indecisive, rehearsing what I was going to say, trying to anticipate my mother's reactions, crying, being confused, feeling alone, frustrated and embarrassed. I felt I was always walking on eggshells. As a codependent son, I found myself being led to and attracted to the seminary. I was a pleaser and found my identity in wanting to heal others and to look good to them. At the time, as a codependent, following the rules, not upsetting the status quo, enjoying religious titles, being a hero to friends, relatives and Catholics was important to me, but only added to my insecurity.`

"You certainly have put a lot of thought into all this, Ray," Danielle said. "I most certainly haven't thought that much about it."

Her comment instantly made me realize just how long I had been thinking about all of it, and the weight of it brought the lump back to my throat. I slowly sipped my coffee before replying.

"Yes, to say I've been thinking and writing about all this for a long time, Danielle, would be an understatement … and now it just flows out of me. The difference now, however, is that it flows smoothly, not like it did for many years … a raging torrent of stuff I didn't understand and couldn't articulate."

With that, we went into another silent period, relaxing, watching other diners come and go. I felt a kind of contentment, even a little joy with the realization of how free we had become of our pasts, and how accepting of them in all their ugliness. After some minutes of this distraction, Danielle began again.

"Before Doug, I never had to live with, and constantly relate to someone that I felt intimidated by and, like I said, the experience started the process of fear growing in me."

That was my queue. I pulled out some more paper and read what I had written about fear: "Abuse is when one person uses fear to control another. Being able to make me afraid of him, the bishop made himself more powerful than me. It is easier to make someone fearful when there are pre-existing power differences that can be exploited, such as being forced to go for counseling, being reprimanded, having to move and, when all of these tactics fail, being forced to go to an institution for rehabilitation."

Danielle nodded as she listened, and then said, "It's amazing how many similar feelings we shared."

"And we have more to unravel," I added.

"And despite 'the look' Doug would give me ... and the way he kept me emotionally detached from him, he expected me to not only respect him, but to love him!" Danielle sighed briefly, and then went on. "It was as if we needed each other. He needed a wife for the children and to take care of the home, and we needed a husband and a father to provide us with shelter and food, and I accepted that ... at least while the children were at home."

"Yes, the dependency!" I continued. "Another way in which priests are similarly kept in line is by being kept in a codependent relationship with the one percent.

Codependency is characterized by control, which denies freedom and is as painful and destructive as any other addiction that is masked by denial. In this addiction, there is a pattern of painful dependence and approval played out in an attempt to find safety, independence and approval, self-worth, and identity."

"Amen to that!" Danielle affirmed with a smile.

"It is an addiction," I went on, "to a supportive role characterized by caretaking, repression, dependency, poor communication, weak boundaries, lack of trust, anger, low self-worth, a devotion to willpower ... and it's all viewed as a sign of loyalty."

"I should have waited a little longer before saying Amen." Danielle interjected.

"And I'm still not done ... The one percent kept me in my co-dependence by constantly reminding me of my duties. They did not like me making waves and wanted me to run a smooth operation, with lots of confessions, converts, committees, organizations and, most importantly, to be financially viable. Attracting the media or giving my own point of view to the media was forbidden. Although they can no longer burn heretics at the stack, if you upset them they can use silencing and banishment."

"Thank God I only had to endure the 'look'," Danielle added. "But Ray, why is there abuse? It sounds like a dumb question, but why does it happen in the first place?"

"No, it's a good question. The issue touches many of us on a very personal level. It has become an overwhelming social problem surrounded by shame and secrecy. The abusers have protected themselves through denial. Denial protects them from ever thinking that what they do, or did, would cause them to feel ashamed."

"For sure," Danielle added. "I could never have seen Doug humbling himself that way or, as you would say, allowing himself to be that vulnerable. That would never happen!"

"When they are challenged to confront their issues," I continued, "abusers take a defensive position, reject the idea, and are not open to change because they are in denial about their abusive behavior. But denial also interferes with them ever understanding the issue.

"The problem I had," Danielle said, "was that I knew Doug could hurt me if he tried, but I didn't know if he actually would if I pushed him too far. Just the fear of him hurting me kept our respective positions clear … but I wasn't happy about it."

As usual, it was a heavy session, so at that point we took a short, much-needed break before I continued.

"As I was saying, Danielle, the abusers cannot look outward, since they are in a state of denial about their behavior. They remain defensive, self-righteous, manipulative, perfectionist, and in control. They see two options: passivity or aggression. Neither involves taking responsibility for their feelings or behaviors. Being accused of being abusive is highly uncomfortable for them and serves to desensitize them to their own behavior."

"So, in other words, had either of us tried to talk about it with our abusers, they wouldn't have known what we were talking about?"

"That's probably true, Danielle. It would be impossible for them to understand, or to have an open mind to what was being said to them because their views of reality were through tainted glasses of denial. That denial was entrenched in their addiction to power and control. Being in denial, they want obedience first. In my case, their goal was to insist that the ninety-nine percent stay in their pews. The one percent is offended at us doing our own thing, by our 'picking and choosing' what we want to do and believe, and they are certainly intolerant of us expressing our own views publicly."

"I often thought of leaving my abuser," Danielle added, "but I kept thinking of the children. I wanted them to have a home life of some sort until they could leave on their own. I knew I could hang in till then, but when the last one was out, I prepared to follow."

"Well, if you can admit to that, Danielle, I'd like to add that I, too, tried to escape a few times from my situation, by taking a year off, but I was trapped in religiosity, clericalism and guilt. I always came back, begging to be accepted, manipulating and assuring the bishop that I was ready to continue. I relied totally on him for my support and survival because I feared being rejected ... although I was accepted back. I felt trapped."

"Like me, I suppose ... What I found so difficult over time was that there was no emotional connection between Doug and me anymore."

"Acknowledging their shadow side is also impossible for abusers when they tend to be emotionally isolated from us and lack intimate and supportive relations with us," I went on. "It is almost impossible to trust and feel intimate with someone when you know that if you cross a boundary with them you will quickly be put back in your place, or when you hear how they have treated your peers, whom they silenced."

"Or how other women were treated when they did cross his boundaries …"

Trivial Demands

*O*ur next session was focused on the demands that we both had experienced coming from our abusers, and their tendency to want to focus everything on themselves.

Danielle began. "I knew it even then, but thinking about all the demands that Doug made on me has made me realize even more how trivial they seemed, and at the same time, how very important they were to him."

"Me too," I said, "I know now that all those things that I had considered trivial at the time were essential to my priesthood, and important to the one percent."

"As I said last time, Ray, I gave up my concern about my own needs and focused on running the home and, slowly, hoped I could re-find my own identity in twenty years when the kids were gone."

"How did you process all that, Danielle," I asked.

"Well, Ray, I looked above …" She smiled at my puzzled look, and went on. "There were a lot of things the children were being taught in religion classes that I considered trivial, but I couldn't say that to them, nor to my husband, so I would tell God what I thought. He made for a great listener."

"Yes, of course ... I can relate to that ... I was the one teaching it. Holding rigid beliefs, the one percent remains defensive and self-righteous. A handout I used in religious education material many times was entitled 'How to create Christians today.' I would hand it out to those who were preparing to enter the Catholic Faith, but upon reading it you soon realized that other Christian denominations could not have used the material. It should have been entitled, 'How to create Catholics Today.' It used the words 'Roman Catholic' and 'Christian' synonymously, and many Roman Catholics think they are synonyms, even though the Roman Catholic Church is just one among hundreds of denominations that make up the Christian Religion. In other words, not all Christians are Catholic, but many of the one percent think they should be."

"I'm sure I saw that pamphlet around," Danielle kidded.

"I sure hope so," I said as I smiled back at her. "I used to hand them out to all my parishioners."

She went on. "Although it was not long before I no longer had an emotional, romantic relationship with Doug, he had his needs met whenever he wanted. I could never 'have sex' outside of a loving relationship ... as a professional, if you know what I mean, but I now have a good idea of how unfulfilling that must feel to those who do. I doubt Doug ever even thought about me getting my needs met. I even wonder if the possibility of my leaving him ever entered his mind. I think he knew that as long as the kids were home, I'd be there, and he was right on that score."

As she sipped her coffee, Danielle continued. "I was out of the community and away from the church until just recently, Ray, but I have wondered how all those sex scandals within the church affected the remaining priests?"

"I don't have contact with any of the parish priests I knew in 2002, before I left ... but I can only imagine how difficult it must have been to be in the parishes with all that going on. In April, 2002, at the Vatican meeting, they used the term 'ephebophilia' to try to make a distinction between what was going on and pedophilia, the attraction to pre-pubescent children. They did that because all the cases involving sexual abuse by priests at the time involved adolescents, so it gave them a way to avoid any mention of 'pedophile'."

"But why did those priests act out sexually against minors of any age?" Danielle asked.

"Enter an important aspect of the shadow side of the priesthood," I replied. "It is a lonely, privileged, prestigious profession, with access to many young boys. Parents welcome having a priest as a chaperone and companion to their boys, but if that same priest were to take a girl out, there would be questions. All the values within the clerical culture are male ... with a spiritual fraternity atmosphere."

"At the time," I explained further. "I wrote that the men who committed those crimes had entered high school seminaries in the 50s while still in their adolescence, before they had dealt with their own issues of intimacy, and before they understood their own sexuality or had ever been in a close relationship, let alone an intimate one. As a result, they emerged immature, both emotionally and sexually, especially after living their youth as obedient, celibate, and chaste young men. When they left the seminary, they again related to adolescents … where they had left off. These men are not homosexuals, and neither are pedophiles as a rule homosexual, yet homosexual priests are made the scapegoats by the one percent … once again."

"Ray, tell me some more about the trivial demands that you experienced."

"What I've come to appreciate much more," I replied, "is that what may be trivial to me can be anything but trivial to someone else. I know that the entire topic around celibacy is anything but trivial to the one percent. The entire male clerical hierarchy is structured on it, but if you were to ask some parishioners what they thought about it … some would wonder why priests can't get married. Others, including many priests, would wonder why it even still exists, and on and on would go the opinions. To some priests, celibacy is trivial, not important to being a priest, irrelevant in this time in history, a burden and an unnecessary sacrifice.

"However," I added, "ask someone among the one percent about celibacy and you will get a very different answer. Words such as "essential," "fundamental," even "sacred" and "holy" are applied. But, for me as a gay man who sought shelter in celibacy but couldn't remain faithful to it … celibacy seemed, trivial."

Danielle laughed as she responded. "I didn't think my question was that complex, but it is helpful for me, too."

"In what way," I asked.

"Okay ... Let me see ... I viewed many of the tasks I did on a daily basis as being trivial demands on me, but to many women, and certainly to my husband, they were important and essential to running the home ... to the point that I should somehow feel honored as an obedient wife to have the privilege of doing them. But when asked of me on a regular basis, those demands seemed trivial, and my doing them was taken for granted. They were so frequent and repetitive that I felt like a robot that couldn't stop for fear that everything would come apart somehow. Doug would say, 'Don't forget to pick up the kids,' as if I would ever forget them, or as if I wouldn't remember unless he reminded me every time. So it got to the point that almost everything he asked me to do, and everything he said to me, became a trivial demand. I couldn't see the phenomenon as being abusive at the time, but when the kids left home and those demands kept coming, I began to see the trees through the forest and started taking steps toward leaving."

"Yes, I can see that," I said. "Your experience reminds me of when, in my youth, I wondered why priests kept asking the congregation for more money, and yet kept building huge buildings that were so expensive to heat. But then, when I became a priest, I started asking for more money, too, the same way that the priests of my youth had done. Why? The cost of church supplies, the vestments, the trimmings, are not seen as obstacles to Christ's vision, nor are they seen as a problem when those involved are all held in an addiction. In our addiction of codependency, we can rationalize that nothing is too good for the Lord. Hence, needing and requesting money is a constant concern and preoccupation for priests."

"You did your share of financial requests, if I remember," Danielle said.

"We had all sorts of programs to get people back into church, which we always said was because we were concerned about their relationship with God, and their salvation, but it was about money, power and control."

"I remember!" Danielle broke in. "I remember you telling us that about the connection between our church attendance and our salvation. In fact, you got me involved in some of those renewal programs shortly after our wedding."

"Ah, yes, of course," I said. It was a matter of striking while the iron was hot! It was important to be convinced ourselves so that we wouldn't feel guilty about what we were doing. In reality, we needed money for our own upkeep, our residences, our salaries, and those of our staffs. We needed money for the upkeep of the buildings, the churches, the halls, and the schools. And the donations needed to be relatively high because a percentage of the collections always went to the bishop's office for his upkeep and his staff and residence, etc. Then there were all the special collections for church charities ... and the needs of the pope, of course."

"Some of us suspected, if we didn't clearly know what it was all about," Danielle added.

"I'm sure," I replied. "Our rationalizing has gone to new heights in this century to justify a lot of things, including the relevance of celibacy."

"Help me understand the connection to celibacy again, Ray," Danielle asked.

"It always comes back to the same issue ... that Jesus was celibate, according to them, and he didn't mess around, so what was good enough for Jesus is good enough for priests ... despite the fact that in the first few centuries most of the one percent and the rest of the clerics were, in fact, married. And St. Augustine, who, before he became a saint, had messed around for years. Then he stopped and told the rest of us not to do all that he had done ... and he was made a saint! And the one percent have listened to his saintly advise ever since. To be a priest, celibacy is a requirement, not a choice."

Danielle chuckled as she took another sip of coffee. "At the same time," she said, "a lot of us made wrong choices."

"And many of us thought celibacy was the right choice," I pointed out, "and others felt they had no other choice. If you wanted to be in the military you had to be straight or gay and not tell, though now you can tell, and stay. To abandon celibacy would upset Rome's foundation and make it harder to control its men. However, when celibacy is not freely chosen, there is inevitably a struggle with issues of intimacy and sexuality. And the biggest sign of the struggle is the pain and depression within the individual. The pain is temporarily alleviated by filling in the gap with materialism, food, alcohol, sex, religion, codependent relationships or a combination thereof."

The intensity of our conversation was once again tiring. We relaxed into relative silence to catch our breath and then finished our meal. Then Danielle reflected, "You know, Doug and I were so busy with our own duties and chores that I began to be grateful that I had his help. From the outside, we looked quite stable … just like many other couples around us. I found out later that a few of my friends in town were going through similar or worse relationships, and yet none of us ever said a word to each other. Seems we didn't trust each other very much or were afraid to try. If someone betrays a trust in a small community, life can be unbearable, and perhaps the abuse can go from subtle to more direct."

"Yes, probably," I said. "You get the message that some things are not to be revealed or talked about. It reminds me of an interview I saw on an American TV program about a group of seminarians preparing to be ordained to the priesthood. All of them claimed to be gay men but had given up those 'urges' to accept celibacy. I felt anger at the institution and sorrow for those men who were suppressing their sexuality and passion for the requirements of the institution, while probably knowing the one percent thought of them as 'not normal' for even being homosexual, of course, was not talked about."

"Your book, *No Longer Lonely,* will probably make some of them think more about that and, maybe, be more open about it."

"I hope so," I said. "When the stress or loneliness begins, their sexuality won't be suppressed for long. They will act out in secret, become asexual, or take up an addiction to mask their human need for sexual expression, as so many priests are now doing. Church teaching has a bias against sexual intercourse and maintains that greater purity is found in celibacy. This conflict is creating a spiritual crisis that is causing homosexuals, including gay priests, to re-evaluate religion and the meaning of their lives."

"Even with the parallels and similarities in our experiences, Ray, it sounds like your issues are a little more complex than mine, yet there is one major thing in my mind that we have in common in all of this."

"That we can talk about it?" I asked.

"True enough," she said. There is that … but I was thinking more about the fact that we both felt like puppets throughout, and not persons, do you know what I mean?"

"I know exactly what you mean, Danielle," I said.

Puppets and Self Doubt

I arrived at the Paddlewheel early for my next meeting with Danielle and pondered the notes I had made after each of our previous discussions. It was truly amazing to me how a gay man, who had been a Catholic priest for many years, had so much in common with a former victim of spousal abuse. Our common experience of being treated like objects instead of human beings was next on the agenda.

"When thinking about our talks," Danielle began shortly after arriving with her lunch tray, "I realized how I did things on autopilot at times, without any feelings or caring, and how Doug treated me as if I didn't actually have any feelings."

"When two people exist together without love and affection, I think they become insensitive to the humanity of each other and, like you said, Danielle, they begin to lack empathy and compassion for each other. It becomes a relationship of convenience. That's exactly how I felt toward my bishops."

"Sad when you think about it, isn't it Ray?"

"It's almost inhuman."

"Those parishioners who sought individual choices … the 'pick-and-choose' Catholics, as we called them … were often given looks of disappointment by me as I tried to convince them that they were thinking wrongly, just as my bishop often tried to tell me I was thinking wrongly, and tried to instill fear in me by yelling at me or shaming me. But parishioners who were ready to leave the church knew better than to argue with those of us in power. And those who did leave did so silently. They didn't want to confront the one percent addicted to power and control, and nor did they want to confront priests who were at the service and obedience of the one percent. After a while, you just became numb and accepted the experience, you gave up your humanity, your right to be a separate human being … You're so right Danielle, it was very sad."

"I remember a term you used before, Ray, that struck me … 'tamed adult'."

"Yes, for sure! You were kept in line in the same way that the one percent tried to keep me in line, by intimidation, guilt, control, and isolation—a tamed adult!"

"Amen! Amen! Amen!"

"A part of the intimidation the one percent uses and, I confess, a tactic that I unconsciously used as an enabler, was that of labeling other people … I referred to it earlier. When you label someone, you minimize them and their behavior; you reduce them to that label. And you justify, rationalize and externalize your own behavior toward them. The one who is labeling another is in denial …

denial that they are imposing their power and control over those they label. Does that make sense, Danielle?"

"Sounds like the bullying we are hearing so much about on the news these days ... that kids are dealing with."

"Exactly! I remember one reporter, writing about the sex scandals in the church, saying that the ninety-nine percent knew few details, besides being asked to 'pray for their sick servants in the Lord.' The reporter said that attempts by the one percent to buy the silence of the victims, and their inability to sympathize and show compassion for them, revealed their abusive power and control over those victims and their local priests. Damage control would have required admission of guilt followed closely by a remedial plan of some sort, but the one percent just waits for the secular press to expose the evil before saying anything at all. I fully agree with what that reporter wrote. As well, I think that when there is no one to support you, you begin to doubt yourself and your own worth. When everyone around you is saying and believing something different than you, you need to be very strong to be able to 'pick and choose' your own beliefs and values."

"That's really tough to do for anyone, priest, abused spouse, or defenseless child," Danielle agreed. "That's exactly how I began to feel about myself ... I had no one to share with and no one to support me."

"Among the ninety-nine percent and among some priests, many do select or 'pick and choose' what they will believe in. The one percent tries to react against the pick-and-choose Catholics. At one time, in the province of Quebec, the one percent, through their priests, would tell people how to vote, and even how many children to have. They had total authority … it was a medieval Catholicism … but those days are gone forever!"

"Not only have those days gone," Danielle added, "but that whole century is gone."

"Nowadays," I said, "a common putdown of a lot of people who still go to church is that many of them only go for the rites of passage, such as baptisms, weddings, and funerals, or for special services such as Christmas and Easter. I think that happens because many simply can't reconcile the official teachings of the institution with their everyday lives."

"I never knew whether my husband actually made the connection or not," Danielle said.

"Many reject the institution's position on sex outside of marriage, along with divorce, abortion, and the use of artificial birth control methods. Many feel that women should be eligible for ordination as priests, and even more feel that priests should be allowed to marry."

"To a male or a female?" Danielle asked with a grin.

"Thank you, Danielle … Young people not only tend to reject the institution's teachings around sex but they are also receptive to couples who are not married, both living together and having children … and they are more tolerant of freedom of sexual orientation. But the one percent only sees that the pick-and-choose Catholics are not doing what it wants them to do."

"That's how I felt with Doug," Danielle added.

"I'm sure … Doug would want you to obey all the rules just as the church wants the 'pick-and-choose' folks to obey all their rules, regulations and obligations of the institution, and to go to church weekly so that the one percent and their priests have a firm financial base in order to continue to maintain buildings and personnel."

"I guess I've always known that," Danielle replied, "but it sounds so diabolical."

"It does ... but the problem is that the one percent, because of denial, is unable to understand and respect individual choices and individual spiritual needs. Instead, members of the one percent continue to demand, 'Our way or the highway!'"

Danielle chuckled. "That certainly sounds like my husband. At the time, I couldn't be objective about what I thought and wanted to do so how could I be confident in deciding what was best for myself. I had made the decision to stay put for the kids, but after them ... when they left, then I'd think about myself. Had I been in a city, I'm sure events would have unfolded differently. Back then, I learned to accept what I had with Doug as a relationship of convenience."

"And what you're saying could easily be said about many priests. No children would be involved, but the learning to defer considerations of oneself in the same way happens all the time. And it doesn't help that the one percent minimizes situations by representing events, such as the pedophile scandals, as being less serious than they actually are by protecting their own clerics and the 'religious' from facing criminal charges, which anyone within the ninety-nine percent would have to face. It takes the media to expose that shadow side."

"And which they do swiftly when they're caught," Danielle added.

"Yes, of course ... and to add insult and pain to the injustice of their actually harboring criminals by protecting the guilty among them, the one percent silences everyone involved. In having their own treatment centers they have been able to police themselves. They use psychiatrists to help them put their pedophile priests back into circulation while keeping it all out of the public eye."

"I hope all that, too, is gone forever, Ray ... and may I add a favorite quote of mine at this point, which I think is appropriate and which I am sure even Mother Theresa would agree with ... 'Celebrate all the things you don't like about yourself ... Love yourself.' That's from Lady Gaga," she said.

And on that note, we sat back and relaxed a good while, just sipping coffee and watching other diners. Our lunchtime sessions had become so very comfortable and routine. The sights and smells of the place had taken on a new warmth and connection as soon as I entered. As we sat, I recalled recently reading a joke that I thought Danielle would appreciate.

"Listen to this, Danielle," I said, breaking our peace and quiet. "I'm sure you will relate ... 'A couple broke up for religious reasons," I said, and then paused before delivering the punch line ... "Although he thought he was God, she disagreed."

Danielle laughed and then said, "But, you know, Ray, there is a sad side to that joke."

"Oh, I'm sure," I said.

"The sad thing is Doug still believes he is God … When I met him, I loved him so much. I thought we would be there for each other and help each other grow as persons and as a couple. It's when I think that I was with a man who didn't even know what that meant that really saddens me. Gradually, as time flashed by and we were both caught up in running the home, I began to wonder what I had gotten myself into … I began to feel alone with him …"

She paused to catch a tear running down her cheek, and then choked out, "It's horrible to feel alone, and lonely, when you're with someone you thought you were in love with."

"I'm sorry Danielle … for bringing still more tears out of you. I know how you felt Danielle. I, too, was surrounded by people and yet felt alone because of my secret and knowing how the one percent would react if I ever shared it."

"Doug was constantly correcting my understanding of whatever he might have said," she added, "or my misunderstanding of what he had meant. It made it hard to feel love, or to even want to be with him."

"I was told what to believe and what to preach," I said. "My interpretations and biases were to be kept to myself. I was to preach the church's official teaching and beliefs only. As a priest, that's what is expected of you, but what began to really surprise me was how little my personal views counted for anything. During my studies, we were encouraged to question and to be analytical, but once ordained, you stuck to the party line, or else."

"Doubting myself," I went on, "started at a very young age, though I didn't understand what was happening at the time, and then it took years of counseling to work it through. I realized that when you're in a relationship that is abusive, one based on power and control, you become an enabler as well as a victim. As with all abuse victims, I think I was unwilling to share or to compromise. And I had been either passive or bullying myself. I lacked confidence in my own abilities and wouldn't try new things unless I knew I would succeed. I had trouble solving problems, so my relationships ended with no closure, especially since I had poor conflict-resolution skills. I found it difficult to maintain an intimate relationship due to issues of trust, disclosure and honesty. I had poor boundary issues and found myself parenting others, not respecting others' privacy or their personal space, and I was reticent about giving personal information … Boy, I was a mess, wasn't I?"

"Well, that was then, for the most part," Danielle said as she put a comforting hand on mine and adding, "I can see why you've taken to writing out a lot of this stuff."

"I think," I added, "that while you're in the kind of relationship you and I were both in, you can't express what's going on very well at the time, partly because, at that point, you don't fully understand yourself just what is going on. But as you speak about your situation with someone who understands your experience, it's as if they are taking off your tinted glasses and you begin to see more clearly and to understand more quickly."

"I think you're right, Ray. And now, through this process, we are confirming our experience to each other and able to move forward without regrets."

"True, Danielle. I'm sure of it. Experiencing abuse deprived me of my right to realize my own potential as a human being. The abuse affected my thinking to the point that I began to think that nothing mattered and I would tell myself things like … 'I can't cope … Others are able to deal with this … What would people think if they knew … There's no way out … If I do things properly, do as my bishop asks, it will be okay … Yeah, right!'"

"I became aware that in the midst of my seemingly constant misunderstanding," Danielle added, "that I was becoming more and more vulnerable to Doug's way of thinking, to how he saw things … Looking back, that's scary to think about."

"Danielle, it's through that process in our minds that many people who are abused become abusive themselves, or remain victimized persons indefinitely. We are very fortunate, you and I, that we were able to leave our situations. Many people feel they cannot, and others don't even realize they are in a relationship that is based on power and control."

"My husband always believed that I respected him and that it was my duty to be obedient to him, and there were times when I wondered if he might be right."

"Sounds familiar," I added. "In the church, those in the one percent feel they are to be respected and obeyed, no questions asked. They feel they are in power by the Will of God and, therefore, they are always in the right.

Hence, they believe that society and our culture are in the wrong … even immoral."

"They may have a point there … at times," Danielle said with a smile.

I returned the grin and continued, "It is their responsibility and divine right to remind us of what God wants us to do, which is essentially the same self-righteous and defensive stance of all who abuse. Rather than argue with that arrogance, many parishioners just leave in silence and anger at being kept in a state of guilt and fear, the purpose of which is to intimidate them into blind obedience. In this scenario, there isn't much room for love and compassion, let alone for justice and respect."

"After a while," Danielle confessed, "I was feeling so trapped and alone that I got really hard on myself and had to be careful not to take it out on others around me who wouldn't have understood."

"That's exactly what I felt … Because of all those feelings of guilt, shame occurs when we can't share our inner selves and we become objects of contempt even to ourselves. A low self-esteem is created because of shaming childhood experiences. From our earliest days, a good way to keep us in line was to shame us in public, either by being scolded or by some form of verbal abuse. Shaming wasn't the best aid to self-esteem but what was more important was the use of control and power in order to make sure we knew to whom we were accountable—who was in charge. Had I been able to figure this out sooner," I added, "I think it would have got me thinking earlier about my situation."

"At times," Danielle added, "I felt I was living with two different people, the one I thought I married and the one I actually lived with … It felt very odd at times."

"In 1945, Carl Jung, a Swiss psychologist, referred to the dark, feared and unwanted side of the human personality as 'the shadow'—the thing a person has no wish to be but which is there in all of us. The shadow side that the one percent does not perceive itself as having is its subtle need for the ninety-nine percent to be faithful servants—obedient, submissive, and grateful for serving Mother Church."

"Like me being the faithful mother and the obedient, submissive wife who is supposed to be grateful for every opportunity to serve … As you put it so well earlier, as if I were serving God himself."

"Exactly! The ninety-nine percent, and me as a priest, are to be non-critical of God's Will as expressed through the wishes of the one percent. The one percent wanted me to see my suffering from loneliness and isolation as making sacrifices for the good of the ninety-nine percent that we priests serve, which, in turn, enables us to be more available as enablers to the addiction of the one percent. Keep in mind, Danielle, that you were among the ninety-nine percent, I was the enabler, and the one percent included our bishop, your shepherd and my Lord … a touch of sarcasm," I admitted. "Sorry about that …"

"Not a problem … I understand," Danielle replied, and went on. "As time passed, I began to feel as if I were spinning my wheels. I actually tried to make sense out of Doug's behavior, which only added to my poor self-esteem. I actually began to think that I was stupid for not being able to figure him out, and I took years of that while the children were at home. And then, once I was able to accept that there was something wrong with his behavior and not mine, I lined up at the exit door."

"It must have been very difficult for him, Danielle, since Doug would have been in denial of his behavior and unable to accept doing anything about it without counseling. Some of my friends, once they got used to the language I used for my relationship within the Catholic institution, would ask me how I had reacted to the relationship while within it. Well, the physical effect was that I was always nervous and anxious and always had a sense that something was about to happen. I was often lethargic, ambivalent, had self-doubt, diminished self-esteem, a sense of powerlessness, and I had stress-related illnesses."

"I also frequently had physical ailments," Danielle said, "and it took years before I understood the connection."

"The social effect was that I was emotionally inaccessible," I said. "I had distorted relationships and, therefore, I had few close friendships and was unable to risk getting to know others intimately. I lacked respect; I continued to smile; I kept my opinions to myself or just shared them with other priests of like mind. It was all really about self-doubt ... that was the biggest impact on me."

"I must say, Ray, that from the outside, you did look sane back then."

"Thanks Danielle," I said as we had a laugh. "Needless to say, it took years of self-analysis, psychoanalysis, retreats, spiritual counselors, and clinical studies, all of which few people can undergo, much less afford. But I had the luxury at the time of being an asset to the church, which needed me in reasonably sane condition to function as an efficient enabler … or as a faithful servant, as the one percent would put it."

"So did all that, the increasing self-doubt and its ramifications go on during your entire relationship, Ray?"

"That it did! Every few years, I would experience a sense of meaninglessness. I'd become depressed, aggressive, and withdrawn all at once. In the language of abuse, I then treated my parishioners the same way … as abusive parents treat their children. I became distant and emotionally inaccessible, just as I felt the bishop was distant, paternalistic, controlling, manipulative, and emotionally inaccessible to me."

"I was the same … I doubted my perceptions of my husband and our situation so much," Danielle said, "that I couldn't gather any critical information about my situation and, therefore, was in no position to make an informed decision while I was with him. I was blind and Doug was in denial … What a couple we made."

"Keep your sense of humor, Danielle," I said.

"You know, Ray, the church only added to the guilt feelings I had for not understanding him and for how I felt toward him as a loving father and husband."

"Sorry about that Danielle," I replied. "I'm sure my sermons on being a faithful spouse and thinking less of oneself didn't help you. As you just mentioned, another form of intimidation used is guilt, always being made to feel unworthy. From the moment of birth, Catholics are taught that we are born with 'original sin'."

I suddenly realized I hadn't tasted anything I had eaten since we sat down, yet my plate was empty, as was my coffee cup, and said to Danielle, "I didn't think it was possible to eat on autopilot."

She laughed and replied, "The concentration and deep memories do take over, don't they?"

Helplessness and Exhaustion

*W*hile all of exhilarating, liberating and fulfilling, my sessions with Danielle were also exhausting for both of us, which brought us to thinking about the exhaustion and helplessness we had felt as victims of abuse so we set that as our next topic for discussion.

The time came quickly and I told Danielle right off that every few years during my priesthood, when I became ill I thought my body was trying to tell me that I was not happy and that I was in an unhealthy situation. But I could not read the signs of my own "dis-ease." But when I read *The Drama of the Gifted Child* and *The Dysfunctional Church,* I became aware of my dysfunction ... and that of the church ... a church I had accepted I would serve faithfully. Yet every few years I became exhausted, felt helpless, and fell into depression.

"That's what happened to me, too," Danielle said in a matter-of-fact tone. "No sooner had I accepted serving faithfully than, a few years later, I was getting depressed ... The parallels in our experiences still amaze me!"

"And leading up to my dis-eases," I went on, "I would become withdrawn, not only from my parishioners, but also from my friends. I became powerless over my relationships. I questioned everything and everyone. I left others out of my life mostly because I didn't know how to include them. Even in a group setting, I felt comfortable with others only when I was in control. Therefore, when my life became difficult, I had no idea how to include others. And worse, I felt I couldn't dare give anyone the impression that I was not in control."

"An out-of-control priest," Danielle said. "That would have gone over well, I'm sure. In my world, I had to stay in control for my children's sake, but it was as if I had an entire community watching me."

"As I went through that time ... I remember trying to live up to the ideal and felt helpless and exhausted and then, of course, I became physically and emotionally vulnerable. At the time, I didn't realize it was the institution that made me feel trapped and powerless. I didn't have any exterior resources that could have helped me, other than the psychologist who merely verified that I was not happy and needed to do something about it."

"And me," she interjected, "with no car and my parents and relatives way off in St. Boniface, and surrounded by Doug's family and friends, I was kept in survival mode and felt completely powerless. To confront him in that environment was just unthinkable."

"Like me ever thinking about confronting the one percent ... it would be perceived as going against the church, which, according to them, Jesus himself had founded. How could I dare go against that? It would have been perceived as heretical. The arrogance, of that idealized image that members of the one percent have of themselves has caused anger among many of the faithful, especially those in minority groups, many of whom have said, Enough! Enough!"

"What do the bishops say about all that now?" Danielle asked.

"They blame and accuse others of being disloyal. They blame their own abusive behavior on an outside force. For instance, every time the Roman Catholic Institution is portrayed as being human, the one percent screams foul! They say the institution is being singled out, that the authors are being anti-Catholic, that there is negative stereotyping, religious bigotry. The term often used is 'religion-bashing'."

"And what do the priests say about that?"

"In the area of church teaching, dissent is unacceptable, as it is in any institution. For many priests, it's difficult to settle into a rigid, conforming system, and yet, many find comfort and safety in such a system, as would any abused partner when criticism is seen as disloyal."

"Gee, Ray," Danielle added, "I wasn't going to say much today in favor of listening and actually tasting my lunch, but it seems I have more to say on the subject than I anticipated."

"That's great, Danielle, because I wasn't really keen on listening exclusively to myself the whole time!"

"Okay then," she went on. "The thought for me of leaving my husband while the children were at home felt overwhelmingly fearful in terms of what could be either said or done to us, or how my departure would affect all of us. It seemed like too much of a risk, too high a price to pay, so I stayed for sake of our joint comfort and safety."

"Priests that are visionary, contradictory, or not seen as part of the group are looked upon as rebels in the church. They are said to be making waves and are not considered to be positive contributors. They are considered as not content to work within the system and trying to make improvements from within. I was often perceived that way ... as displeased and dissatisfied. All of those terms were meant to explain away people like me, who are eventually asked to capitulate or to move on. And as the years pass, and as priests we see some of our peers being asked to leave or being transferred to other diocese, we understand the price we will pay for making waves."

"When priests got together, wasn't there ever talk about needing change?"

"Even the thought of needing a fundamental restructuring affecting the one percent or doing things differently was, and still is frightening and threatening for many priests and parishioners, especially for those who are held within the addiction of power and control."

"Why couldn't priests feel comfortable about talking about this among themselves?"

"To be creative you need a safe environment to share your vision. But, it is not safe to speak of married or gay clergy and women priests in a system that has to defend its power and control, and uses silencing to ensure obedience and faithfulness. If priests are perceived as disloyal to the Roman Catholic Institution, public shaming and condemnations are used to ensure orthodoxy. If institutions for rehabilitation are unable to reprogram or rehabilitate offenders, then efforts are made to ostracize."

"But today," Danielle pointed out, "gay men are accepted and seen as assets in many professions."

"That's true, Danielle," I said, "but when my self-esteem and confidence were weak and vulnerable, I was easily controlled. Add to that, someone who is creative and sensitive, as many gay men are, and you have a priest who is experiencing a great deal of frustration and anxiety within a patriarchal, self-righteous, homophobic institution."

"It's also sexist considering that most church volunteers are women and not in positions of power," Danielle added.

"And, I truly believe, that is also why gay men are attracted to the priesthood in the first place, and why the one percent tries to perpetuate a system of male, homophobic, celibate priests in the image of Jesus. The irony being that it's doubtful Jesus was homophobic.

"As beautiful as the town was and as caring as most people were, Ray, I too was isolated from any kind of a support group that could help me out, especially without my in-laws and his friends finding out."

"In early 1992, because of the media coverage of a serial pedophile priest, who was later murdered in prison while serving his sentence, the pope spoke out. He asked that the training of priests include franker discussion of sexuality and celibacy. Then, in March of that year, he asked for an overhaul of seminary programs because of a lack of candidates and rising clergy burnout. He insisted on education, training, and character development, with the key components being an understanding of one's own sexuality, the capacity to relate to others, and for seminaries to present chastity in a manner that showed an appreciation and a love for that concept. The reaction of some seminaries, as you might guess, was simply to tighten their admission requirements and to watch their seminarians more closely."

"Wow! That would have sealed the fate of the traditional one percent," Danielle said with a smirk.

"In the past, celibacy was described as a gift we give in order to live out a life-long service to others as a call from God. We were meant to be celibate men, working to build a kingdom here and now. Today, celibacy is described as a life without sexual activity of any kind, including masturbation."

"Well, that should attract more men to the priesthood," Daniel said with obvious sarcasm.

"Priests will have sexual feelings, but they are not to put themselves in 'situations' and they are to pray for strength."

"I wonder if men pray daily for that grace," she added.

"As for me Danielle," I replied, "I prayed like hell. Celibacy is a radical call and the priest makes a decision not to act on his desires, which, may I add, were given to him by God."

"Has the abuse of children ended?"

"The one percent cites the apparent fact that fewer cases of sexual abuse occurred during the 1990s as evidence that their new screening and training was successful. However, I believe that despite the new screening and training, a disproportionate number of gay men remain in the closet. Abusive priests have just become more careful."

"And denial lives on," Danielle added.

"And denial lives on, Danielle."

Occasional Indulgences

*J*he topic of our meeting had Danielle feeling down before we even started.

"It was the unhappiest subject for Doug and me," she said upon getting comfortably seated. Revisiting the subject now makes me realize just how painful a relationship can be without love. Even my children ask me, now that we all live in the city, why I stayed in the marriage. They saw that we didn't seem to love each other. They tell me they would see couples on TV, or even some of their friends' parents and could tell that their relationships were different than what they saw with their own parents. They couldn't understand it at the time, partly because there wasn't any physical abuse between Doug and me, and their father went out of his way for them, attending sports activities and parent events. They could tell there was something wrong between their parents but didn't have the words to articulate it. As they grew older, apparently they talked between themselves and decided they didn't want to be in a relationship like ours when they got married themselves ... How sad to think of your parents that way."

"In the years since, Danielle, as you shared your experience with other women, I am sure you began to see you were not in the minority in how you felt ... probably quite the contrary. And that's what is really sad for me. As a priest, I would hear countless confessions of unfaithfulness and regrets from people, but what could I say to them in a two-minute confessional?"

"When we first got married," she added, "we made a point of remembering our birthdays and anniversaries, and we'd be affectionate and try to do something for each other, or with each other. But as time passed, the kisses stopped and the gifts were forgotten, even at Christmas. Now I hear that the children saw all of that and felt sad for us. It had to affect them. In the support groups I attended, people often referred to the children as the biggest victims of such a relationship. Thankfully, mine have become strong survivors and good, loveable young adults themselves. Go figure!"

"I'm absolutely convinced that it was your prayers and faith in God that protected all of you, Danielle," I said.

"But what did we, as parents, teach them about a loving Father?"

"Forgiveness, patience, sacrifice, selflessness, and even faithfulness, probably ... They were good children, as I recall, and you were both kind and caring parents. You both did what you could, and in the only the way you knew how. You were the parents they needed for their spiritual journey. One day they may understand even more fully and move beyond reconciliation. Doug's power and control over you was subtle, as we've talked about. He wouldn't explode when you expected him to. It wasn't as overt as it is with some husbands, who make a show of flowers and chocolates until their next explosion."

"They would have been nice to get," Danielle said, fighting back the tears.

"But had you received them in that situation, the gifts would have been meaningless, as they are to so many women who do receive them."

"Why does it have to be like this, Ray?"

"In part, because both people at the beginning of the relationship don't make a conscious effort each day to think of the other … every day … for the entire time they are together. I was the one who performed the marriage ceremony so you weren't listening to me when I asked you, and countless other couples, to remember on every anniversary the same Scripture passage you had chosen for your wedding. The day couples stop thinking of each other with love is the day the marriage becomes only one of convenience."

"You sound like you're still a priest, Ray."

"I still feel like one, Danielle … According to Psalm 110 Verse 4, I'll always be a priest. But I feel and believe that I'm in the same loving relationship with a God of divine intelligence and infinite presence, whose presence and love are as real for me now as they were when I was a priest serving a God that I addressed as Father."

"Unlike that kind of father, my husband had a way of looking at me and the children," Danielle replied, "that would make you freeze on the spot. None of us dared cross him, and when we tried we were put in our place very strongly. So when I knew I had upset him about something that I may have said, or didn't say, or something I did, yet he did not give me that look, I would feel even more responsible for the times that I did get it ... Now, if that doesn't mess with your self-esteem and self-worth, I don't know what does. It took me years to work through all that."

"Yes, I know it takes years, Danielle, and I can hear that you have worked through a lot."

"When I read your book, Ray," she replied in an attempt to lighten the mood a little, "I knew we could talk about all this. I just didn't know there would be so much salad involved." After a brief laugh she added, "For you, Ray, were there more good times than bad times, or not?"

"That's a very interesting question because the answer is what kept me in the priesthood. In difficult times of dis-ease, I was offered time out with holidays, medical treatments and retreats. I was given counseling, psychological evaluations, and permission to start projects that interested me. Most of those occasional indulgences or little gifts were very subtle. They reinforced my sense of responsibility, and their offer or lack of it, put the bishop in a very omnipotent position relative to me. The contrast between the good and difficult times was so extreme at times that it gave me an exaggerated sense of how good the good times really were, and I, therefore, felt even more invested in the relationship between the one percent and myself."

"Interesting," Danielle reflected. "I can say that my good times all revolved around Doug being a good provider and supportive to the children. There was little physical affection towards myself or the children, so the children's happiness became mine, and it was in their happiness and security that I invested in the relationship. And since I had a diminished sense of self-worth, the little effort he put into our relationship didn't count for much as far as I was concerned."

"I can relate to that, too, Danielle. Even though the one percent was offering me all these occasional indulgences, the power and control over me overshadowed any sense that they were doing all that because they cared about me as a person. It was more because they were concerned about the investment that they had made in me and were concerned about how many more years of obedient service they could get out of me. Finally, I found it impossible to respect the one percent with whom I feared being in a relationship. The fear of being rejected and the fear of what I would do if I left hounded me. So anything they did 'for' me was regarded as more for them than for me, though I was very grateful for the interventions and permissions."

"When our last child left home," Danielle went on, "I could feel my shackles unlock. Doug's efforts at indulgences toward the children, who were on their own, were meaningless for me at that point. He had nothing to offer that would entice me to stay, and I saw the last child's leaving as my sign to get out as well."

At that point, we had but one more topic on our list to discuss, which would have to do with all the supports and resources we had built up in our lives since leaving our abusive relationships in order to move beyond reconciliation, including whatever new relationships we had, and how we now related to our God.

This topic is discussed in Part 3: Moving Beyond Reconciliation.

PART 2

Fifty Years
Too Late

Further Reflections

*I*n an abusive domestic relationship, the male is usually the abuser, the female is the one abused, and the children are the victims. In my experience as a priest, the male, the abuser, is the hierarchy of the church, the one percent. The female, the abused, is represented by the priests. And the children, the victims, are the parishioners who make up the ninety-nine percent.

Using the analogy of domestic abuse helped me understand my journey. It allowed me to move on with no regrets or resentment, and to realistically understand the political reality of the one percent.

In the first part of this book, Danielle and I shared how we both experienced living in abusive relationships, and how we both transitioned out of those relationships. Although many priests may be able to relate to the areas of abuse mentioned in Part 1, many will not be able to see their experience as one of abuse. Either out of denial or, being consciously aware of the position they are in, they will be unable or unwilling to leave that subculture. The price of doing so would be too high and I, for one, totally understand.

For many, winning a lottery would give them the financial resources they would need to be able to leave. And for many others, even with millions in lottery winnings, the price of leaving a ministry of service to the ninety-nine percent, whom they love, would be too much to pay. This, too, I totally understand.

For me, spirituality is about becoming consciously aware of the balance/harmony that is required within ourselves, between ourselves, and with our Higher Power ... whatever we understand that to be.

This view can enable students to live one day at a time while dealing with bullying, sexual expectations, body image, self-acceptance, rejection, and peer-pressure. It also enables adults and some youth to live with addictions, cancer, HIV/AIDS, disabilities, rejections, losses, and changing lifestyles. All of us, no matter what age, color, nationality, creed, or religion, deal with challenging transitions in our lives.

Danielle once asked me, "Ray, do you think change will ever happen?"

I believe change will never happen for many marginalized in the Catholic Institution: women who want to be priests and homosexuals in general, especially gay priests and lesbian nuns. These groups threaten the hierarchy's idealized image and, therefore, are rejected by the one percent, which tries to convince their faithful to do the same.

As for sexual abuse, the Vatican sees clergy sexual abuse as part of a broad societal problem, not as a reflection of structural problems within the church.

For gay priests it must be very painful to have to read from the pulpit some of the directives from the Vatican. For example, the Vatican asked pastors to clearly promote the correct moral teachings of the church and to publicly reprimand individuals who spread dissent.

Church leaders insist that the ordination of women is theologically off limits, but it could be changed if a pope were so inclined. Since the shadow side has not been acknowledged at a conscious level, it has become very dangerous because denial is still used by the one percent in the face of a wide variety of addictions and scandals of which only the tip of the iceberg has been seen so far.

It is only when we are able to say "Enough!" that we are prepared to transition emotionally, physically and spiritually.

Within ourselves

The Fish Bowl:

*J*immy had four pet goldfish that his parents bought him for his ninth birthday. Every night before he went to bed, he would watch the delicate, orange-coloured fish swim round and round in the small glass bowl.

One day, Jimmy noticed that the water in the bowl looked kind of cloudy and the glass was covered with a light film. Jimmy's mom explained to him that what he saw was natural and that the goldfish bowl just needed to be cleaned.

Jimmy knew how to clean the bowl. He had seen his friend Howie do it. He filled up his bathtub with water and put his hand in it to ensure it was the same temperature as the water in the bowl. Then he gently lowered the bowl into the tub until the four goldfish swam out of it and into the tub, where they waited for the housecleaning to be completed.

Later, as Jimmy knelt by the bathtub to retrieve his goldfish, he saw a strange sight. Even though the bathtub was over four feet long and three feet wide, the four goldfish were swimming round and round in a tiny circle, right where Jimmy had originally placed them.

"Mom," yelled Jimmy, "come and look at the goldfish."

Jimmy's mom came into the bathroom to see what all the fuss was about.

"Why are the fish swimming in a little circle when they have a whole tub?" Jimmy asked.

Jimmy's mom smiled at her son and answered, "Because they don't know they are in the tub. They think they are still at home in their tiny glass bowl. That's what they are used to."

We are often not that different from Jimmy's goldfish. Even when we're offered an opportunity to change and grow we decide, instead, to remain living the way we have been, within the same little boundaries, swimming in our same little circles. We choose the familiar over the unfamiliar, the old over the new. We get attached to staying in our comfort zone and we resist taking risks and flowing with the changes that would force us to face the unknown.

And, sometimes, even when life makes those changes for us, like those goldfish, we stubbornly try to hang onto our old realities and fight the transformation that is already taking place.

Living in a fish bowl offered me security and safety, but I wasn't happy because I wasn't free. My "experience" had been that of an abused person who had lived under the power and control of others. That experience taught me how to survive and how to relate to others through the same defence mechanisms that were used on me. Being treated like a child or an object was minimized as being less serious than what I claimed. Having adults in my life denying that they had said a certain thing resulted in my refusing to admit to things that I had said and done ... with a free conscience. I lived according to the example that was shown me.

As a child and teen, I was told what to believe and I had to go along with it or, as I feared, be rejected. I felt helpless in that I did not know who to talk to, and I was made to believe that there was something wrong with me and I was just being difficult, again.

Deep in my heart, I believed that God was truly a loving God and that he/she/it couldn't care less if I believed all that was being said about him/her/it.

I had my parents' religion and mirrored their involvement in their traditions when I was growing up. The rituals of those traditions became part of our family's culture, sometimes with symbols, such as our family Bible and maintaining burial plots. We learned certain hymns, worship styles, ideas, role models and lifestyles.

Being accepted into the seminary seemed a natural fit for me. I was a good person, obedient, submissive, religious, and I enjoyed learning and studying. However, in her book, *The Drama of the Gifted Child*, Alice Miller writes: "If both spiritual hunger and dependency on human loving are denied or rejected, the only thing left is narcissism."

During my first three years of seminary study I was allowed to return home for Christmas, Easter, and summer. If I didn't have a summer job, the staff would find one for me on campus. While away from home, I was able to express myself more; I became more confident and a freer thinker. Upon arriving home, my mother saw my enthusiasm and how I was talking a lot. After the initial update, she went back to her ironing and the conversation was over. By that time, my father was back in front of the television.

I would soon get bored just sitting around home, and would say that I was going out. My mother would give me her "look" and say, "You're going out already; you just got here."

I heard that every time I went home. If I said "no" to something I didn't want to do, or if I did something differently, she would always say, "I don't know why you bother coming home because every time you come back you're worse."

She felt that I was becoming more opinionated, independent and, in her view, rebellious ... and she was right.

I lived in a "fishbowl" for the first fifty-eight years of my life. During that time, I doubted my own experiences and lived the expectations of others.

Abuse can be defined as a union based on one person having all the power and control. I learned how to be obedient to the expectations of others, and I was well disposed to having the power and control wielded by my mother passed on to an institution that really knew how to use it as well.

Although I was able to convince myself that my reasons for entering the seminary were about self-sacrifice, the glory of God and service to his people, my sub-conscious was thinking that this would be the perfect scenario: Mother would be proud, God would take my fantasies away, I wouldn't have to worry about girls any more, and I would get away from home and have a worthwhile job that would please God.

Although I had knowledge about who I was and what my personality traits were, I did not have a heart-felt experience of my own feelings and emotions because I was not living in freedom. My knowledge could not be integrated into a heartfelt passionate experience. My relationships were superficial, since I had not attained an intimacy within myself that would allow me to be honest with myself, let alone with others. I was in denial of what was happening to me, and fearful of being rejected. That was my experience as an abused person.

I have struggled with internal confusion most of my life. I was made to believe that my thoughts and perceptions were wrong because others didn't agree, or because institutions taught something different. As a child, I doubted my tendency for questioning everything. As a teen, I doubted my experience of sexual fantasies and desires. As a priest, I doubted my experience of being misunderstood, of being a free thinker. Why?

Out of their experience as a victim, an abused person cannot relate to words such as freedom, vitality, intimacy, certainty, confidence, self-respect, harmony, true self, spontaneity, honesty, integration. Abused people are constantly second guessing themselves, being belittled, being made to feel they are in the wrong and are inferior.

In 2002, when I attended a workshop on domestic abuse, everything being said about an abused person applied to me. For the first time in my life I had words that related to my experiences, to my feelings and my emotions as a child and as a priest.

For the first time, I knew why I had not been happy. I could relate a lot of what was being said to my own relationship with my mother, but the most striking revelation was yet to come. The insight I gained from that workshop gave me the language I needed to understand why it would be so difficult for me to leave my abusive situation, and why I felt so ambivalent about so many things.

I needed to know that I was not defined by my experience of abuse. Through the language of domestic abuse I began to recognize who I was dealing with. It became clear that the one percent had use of me as long as I was kept in line. Step outside their boundaries and I would quickly be put back in my place, even if it took trying to reprogram me to do so.

As an abused person, my need was to understand the trauma of abuse that I experienced during my life. I needed to realize that I could not be blamed and held responsible for the expectations that others had of me. I was not a bad priest, and I could have been happier with the parishioners had I been treated like an adult and not as a child making waves. Being treated like a child made me aware that my unhappiness had more to do with a dissatisfied abuser and the institution than it did with my being unfaithful to the message of Jesus.

I struggled with worrying what others would think and say if they knew about my sexual orientation, about how I was treated as a priest, and about what I no longer believed in. I struggled with the state of guilt and shame that I kept my parishioners in while not believing in much of what I was being asked to preach. I stayed in the clerical subculture hoping that the situation would get better … and out of a sense of responsibility.

As I pondered leaving, I feared the unknown, not knowing what else to do, the loss of community, a lack of money, not wanting to let others down, and what others would think.

I was always very fortunate in the resources I had "outside of myself." During my studies in 1995 in pastoral counselling, I was able to articulate my spiritual questions. My mentors gave encouragement and support as I spoke about my desire to move beyond religiosity to spirituality. O'Murchu's book, *Reclaiming Spirituality*, has since given me the language I needed to articulate my spiritual experience.

From 2002 to 2004, I was grateful for the resources that were already in place for me, and for those that the correctional institution offered. Those resources allowed for the end to the cycle of abuse that I had been experiencing, not at the hands of the Catholic Church, which is ninety-nine percent "faithful" people, but rather by the one percent.

Since I had been controlled from the outside by fear and guilt, my religious life isolated me from free thinkers who were seen as dissenters. I needed a number of things:

- Information about what was available outside of my present situation, and about what to anticipate before, during, and after leaving.

- The affection, encouragement, support, and time of friends, family and acquaintances ... at least one other person who would be a positive support so that I wouldn't feel alone, as I had often felt in the past.
- Support groups, and a counsellor to mentor me through the transition.
- Legal advice, financial assistance, material assets.
- A safe place to live.
- To continue to take care of my physical, mental, and spiritual health.
- The commitment and belief that I could make the transition and form a concrete plan of action that would give me affirmation and support to go through with it.

To be healthy I need to take care of myself, to listen to my feelings, and to honestly confront my inner emptiness and longing for love. For me to know who I am at any given moment, I need to get in touch with my feelings and emotions. My feelings give me a sense of self and connect me with my wishes and wants. My emotions give me an identity, strength and self-esteem, and are the seeds of my freedom and vitality. My feelings establish my identity, which is the mystery of my heart.

Self-knowledge is an intimate emotional understanding. As Alice Miller wrote, for me, as a narcissistic person, I needed to learn self-respect, which involved a deep listening and knowing of the feeling self.

And although my experience was hurtful, it was not destructive. I would never denounce religion, nor be anti-religion. All the events and experiences that I had, and the positive energy that I have always had and believed in, have allowed me to survive physically, emotionally and spiritually. I have also been given the support, empowerment, and healing necessary to integrate and celebrate my freedom.

Between ourselves

With the one percent:

The one percent, in holding authority, status and wealth, are ensured power over their priests and the ninety-nine percent. They hold authority because of our willingness to submit to them.

As part of the ninety-nine percent, and then as part of the clerical subculture, I would never have even considered questioning the authority of the one percent because I was totally convinced that what the one percent said was part of their duty to ensure the "True Faith" and protect the "Chair of Peter" (the papacy). The idea of questioning any of that would have been seen to be heresy, an irrevocable one-way ticket to hell ... even though Galileo was pardoned and allowed "out of hell" by the same authority.

When I was studying Clinical Pastoral Education to apply for a chaplaincy position, I was doing my internship in both a hospital and a correctional facility. I didn't have to deal with what I perceived to be the demands and pettiness of parish politics.

While I was in parish ministry, I often reflected upon the need for change because of the tensions that existed between the demands of the one percent and the ritual needs of the people, and my own feeling of frustration and helplessness in being at the service of both.

While within the addiction of power and control by the one percent, I experienced being an abuser by being an enabler to the one percent. In that relationship with the one percent, I was also the one being abused, and especially as a gay priest, I was also being victimized by the one percent.

As a priest, I was also sustained by an addiction to co-dependency. It was made clear that I was a chaplain only because the bishop was allowing me to be one.

Whenever a priest or nun had difficulty coping with some aspect of the Catholic Institution and fell into an addiction in order to cope, the one percent had this system in place to protect themselves and their interests. Whenever an intervention was needed in our lives to help us get "reprogrammed" in order to live a healthy, holistic life as an obedient celibate, we were sent to an institution for rehabilitation … and we were forced to go. The only free choice we had was to leave the religious life and find a job elsewhere. For a man or woman in his or her mature years, who had been programmed throughout their life to live in submission, obedience and celibacy that "choice" was strongly in favour of the one percent and their getting their own way … again!

Since people are more literate than in medieval days, they are less inclined to blindly accept what authority says simply because authority has said it. For the one percent to expect blind obedience, or to say that in obeying them, one was obeying God, just doesn't work today. The one percent is being seen for what it is, a group of corporate heads of a very wealthy institution, which uses and tries to monopolize God.

The one percent continues to ignore the fact that the majority of Catholics are not much for the credibility of the Catholic Institution's teachings if the vast majority of its members think, judge, and act as though the norms don't really exist. In looking at the subjective state of mind of the Catholics in my parishes who practised contraception, quite clearly in good conscience, it follows that if their consciences were clear, they were not committing a sin. They most certainly were not confessing what they were doing as a sin. For this kind of thinking not to succeed, the one percent, through the obedience of its priests, has to keep the ninety-nine percent in guilt and shame to maintain its position.

The one percent only see that these pick-and-choose Catholics are not doing what they want them to do. They want them to obey all the rules, regulations and obligations of the institution and to go to church weekly so that the one percent and its priests have a firm financial base in order to continue to maintain buildings and personnel.

Those seeking individual choices are given looks of disappointment as the one percent tries to either convince us that we are thinking wrongly, or to instil fear in us by yelling or shaming. Hence, those who are ready to leave the church know better than to argue with those in power.

I now understood why the one percent is so fearful. Collectively, it can only listen and accept someone who is totally submissive and obedient, and who can be kept in line.

The one percent wants to be respected and obeyed. They feel they are in power by the will of God and, therefore, they are in the right. They feel that society and our culture is immoral, and that it is their responsibility and divine right to remind us of what God wants us to do, which is also the self-righteous and defensive stance of all who abuse. Rather than argue with this arrogance, many are leaving in silence and anger at being kept in guilt and fear in order to be intimidated into blind obedience. In our early history, popes and governments worked together, and then came the separation of church and state. In our century, the one percent could influence the number of children a family should have, who to vote for, and state that sex was only for procreation in a family context between a man and a woman. Concerning remarriage, the one percent has had to allow annulments, or even fewer financial supporters would sit in churches.

If a bad marriage couldn't be annulled, the man and woman involved would be kicked out of the church. There isn't much room for love and compassion, yet alone justice and respect.

Signs were there in 2002 that indicated that something was about to happen. I was hearing how a number of priests and nuns were not allowed to speak out publicly. The most painful example was that of Sister Jeannine

Gramick and Father Robert Nugent, who had worked for decades in ministry with gay and lesbian Catholics. The Vatican, in silencing them and no longer allowing them to minister to homosexual people, was discriminating in the worst kind.

The one percent keeps using "scandal" as a reason for its persecution of theologians and others. Yet studies show that more people were scandalized by the actions of the one percent than by those who supposedly caused scandal.

Despite the fact that Nugent spoke on "silent witness" and Gramick drew on official church documents for the right of church members to speak their opinions and to form their consciences, their arguments were refuted by the 1% and they were silenced. This came as a great disappointment but no surprise to me. It is the inevitable consequence for anyone (abused spouse or priest) who tries to confront the abuser, especially if the abuser is homophobic as well.

Many priests can relate to the pain of having no one to speak to about the feelings of isolation, humiliation, helplessness, fear and vulnerability. Many of us have seen the impact on others. Many of us have been silenced and have seen how the situation has affected our thinking. Yet the Vatican doesn't hesitate to sanction apparent dissenters to its position on celibacy, premarital sex, homosexuality, contraception, euthanasia, creation-centred spirituality, and other issues. Dissent from its official teaching on moral issues is severely censured.

The one percent remains in denial by labeling all gay priests as potential pedophiles in order to entirely avoid the topics of homosexuality and women in ministry. But these issues will not go away, even if some among the clergy and the ninety-nine percent do move on.

So why is there abuse? The issue touches many of us on a very personal level. It has become an overwhelming social problem because it is surrounded by shame and secrecy. The abusers have protected themselves by using denial, which protects them from ever thinking that what they do should cause them to feel any shame. When they are challenged to confront their issues, they take a defensive position, reject the idea, and are not open to change because they are in denial about their abusive behaviour. Unfortunately, their denial interferes with them ever understanding the issue.

To confront the one percent would be perceived as going against the church, which, according to them, Jesus himself founded and, therefore, such a confrontation would be perceived as heretical. The arrogance of this idealized image that the one percent has of itself has caused anger among many of the faithful, especially those in minority groups, who have said, "Enough!"

My present experience is very new to me. I've never experienced freedom before. Using the analogy of the fishbowl, when dumped into a tub of water I swam beyond my familiar and secure social context. I was literally in uncharted waters. I wasn't afraid because I have always enjoyed moving beyond boundaries, evidenced by my readily taking on new parishes and projects. But in all my parishes and projects, the one percent would soon make their presence felt through their expectations and additional boundaries. Their religiosity stifled me and prevented me from feeling happy and free.

It is my observation and experience that the one percent, through no ill-will on their part, is incapable of accepting the gifts of the language of the heart, passion and imagination that women and gay priests could offer the institution. Why? Because the one percent is collectively in the mindset of an abuser and, hence, remains in denial. Members of the one percent can only "listen to and accept" someone who is totally submissive and obedient to them, and whom they can keep in line.

With The Enablers; the subculture of priests:
The Catholic Institution is attracting fewer applicants to the priesthood, and the individuals that it is attracting often mirror the ones already there. As in my case, they are often individuals who have addictive personalities, who accept blind obedience, who tolerate superiors imposing their power and authority upon them, and who interpret this co-dependent situation as serving the will of God. It may be spoken of as "blind obedience," but submissiveness to the control of others is also a typical response of co-dependent persons.

The problem is worsened by the fact that many of these co-dependent persons are also known to be very orthodox and traditional.

As a priest, feelings of guilt, shame and failure would be my fate if I didn't "measure up" to being a disciple of Christ, another Christ in the world, a model of Christian life, a leader of the community, a good priest. Even while still in the seminary, I, along with many others, were aware of the abuse of authority that went on, but with only a few years of studies left, and waiting to "get out on good behaviour," I did not feel that it would be worth it to battle over the issues. I felt I could make a difference once I got out into the real world where everything would be better … not as dysfunctional as it seemed to be in the seminary. I naively thought that I would not be dealing with as many issues of power and control, denial, addiction, issues of authority and expectations. However, the reality turned out to be a case of "out of the frying pan and into the fire."

I actually had not seen the situation I was in as "abusive," and I was unaware of the signs and the dynamics of the addiction. At the time, I was not in touch with what was actually taking place in my life, and in the lives of those around me. I continued to see the one percent and the situations I was and had been in as being better than they actually were or, at least, not as bad as they seemed.

Through a book called *Canon Law*, the one percent maintained co-dependency through laws and regulations around every aspect of what a Catholic cleric and lay person was to think, believe, and do. It has been quietly and uncritically accepted by the ninety-nine percent membership.

This struggle by the one percent to maintain power and control was emotional and psychological abuse, which forced priests to either remain as enablers within the institution, or to leave it altogether, which played on guilt and shame.

I remember an incident in which I told the bishop how the parishioners were indifferent and complaining about what I was trying to do. He looked at me and said, "Remember, Ray, you are their shepherd, and as their shepherd, you are the only one standing on two feet."

I couldn't believe that he had said that. I left his office shocked and scandalized. I then realized that he was considered to be my shepherd, too, and therefore, when I was before him, I was on all fours.

The women "pillars" and the sisters could easily have administered all of the communities in which I served. They were respected and involved in the daily lives of the people. Tensions occurred with the battle of the sexes because at the heart of the addiction of the Roman Institution is a male homophobic need to control women, and to retain its own authority. Priests, as enablers for the one percent, are drawn into this addiction.

With the ninety-nine percent:

In hearing many stories about people with addictions, often someone would refer to the power and control of the church and the pain that it had caused them. Many of us know from personal experience that addicts become the last to admit and accept their addictions. Addicts acquire a dualistic way of thinking in which they can say one thing, do another, and rationalize themselves out of any situation or behaviour.

At the end of an interview, a few bishops have said to me, "Repeat what I just said and I'll deny it." They didn't seem to have a problem in saying something like that. That stance enabled them to say whatever they wanted, and if it ever embarrassed or intimidated into a compromising situation, they simply denied it all, with not a qualm of conscience.

Priests often got talks about the importance of feeling a fraternal collegiality among ourselves. This fraternity was also to include the bishop, who needed to remind us that he was just one of us. Yet, you never dared cross him or this "brother" would show his true colours, red being the dominant one!

Since many priests felt distant and suspicious of each other, there was little confidence and trust among us, and even less so with our bishops. It is not surprising that we were usually not informed, nor was our opinion solicited when we were about to be re-assigned. All the isolation fostered abusive behaviour.

I have stood before a bishop and listened to him while he gave me my next assignment also tell me about the authority that he held, and the obedience that was required of me. Sometimes I was consulted, but usually merely told when and where I was being sent.

Because of isolation, we would not get any contradictory information from anywhere. When made to believe that what I was taught came from God himself, and that my bishop was the spokesperson for God, I didn't have need of anyone else's opinion. I was dependent on my bishop and felt further degraded by my dependence on him.

As an abused priest, I viewed myself as not worth the effort it would take to leave the ministry. The brainwashing worked in the past but today we are becoming better educated and more aware of the dynamics of abuse in every aspect of our lives, and we are saying "Enough!"

Sometimes, when we are asked to describe ourselves, we do so by our roles ... student, teacher, mother, carpenter ... priest. I have worn a mask and fitted into groups and lived up to expectations to the point that I didn't know who I was, and neither did anyone else. My self-esteem was poor and my values, behaviour and beliefs were determined by others. I felt as if I was in prison, locked up and living other people's lives.

Going through all those feelings affected my thinking to the point I wondered what people would think if they knew how I was being treated. I would convince myself that I would try harder to do things properly, according to what others expected, and then everything would be okay. But often I felt there was no way out, that I had to learn how to make the best of it. And then I would soon make waves and the cycle would begin again. I felt caged. It often took all the energy I had to just cope with the moment.

When you're being accused of something by parishioners, or being told by others what they expect of you, or you're confronted by a bishop about making waves, or you're an assistant having to go along with a pastor who should have been put out to pasture long before, your energy gets drained. Through those times I have felt all of ashamed, angry, sad, helpless, confused, betrayed, hurt, stupid, frustrated, overwhelmed, lonely, fearful, paranoid, and tired.

Indeed, maintaining my priestly lifestyle drained me of a great deal of energy and caused me to get physically ill about every five years. The first time was shortly after being ordained. My body felt like it was giving up its freedom and vitality. The reality was that I was becoming a "tamed adult."

My experiences of not being happy, of feeling boxed in, of living sinfully as an active gay male, of not believing in many things within my religious faith, of feeling helpless and misunderstood made me feel I was in the wrong and that God was displeased with me.

When you are in an abusive relationship, you doubt your own experiences. When you are brainwashed, you are convinced that what you think and need are not as important as what your abuser wants you to think and believe. It was only when I was out of the abusive situation that I could recognize the abuse and begin to articulate my experience and have it validated.

The one being abused is "kept in line" in the same way that the one percent tried to keep me and the parishioners in line—by intimidation, guilt, control, and isolation. We were kept busy with programs and services and we got tired of that because it was always the same people doing everything. If few participated, or if something failed, I was blamed.

The relationship between the one percent and my parishioners was also one of economic abuse through withholding the basic needs that the parish had, such as wanting to build or repair something with "their" money, but which was under the control of the one percent through me.

As abusers, the entire hierarchy was, and still is, in a state of denial of its addiction to control and power. They could only see me as a "problem" to be dealt with, just as any abused partner would be dealt with in order to keep him or her in line. I either "fit in" and was accepted, or I didn't "fit in" and simply could not be accepted.

I had taken many self-awareness programs, but related them back to my role and responsibilities. I was considered a free spirit, which had to be offered up in order to accept a life of commitment and obedience. Being sexually active had to be offered up in order to live a celibate chaste life. The programs were helpful in helping me to try to live as a priest, but who was I if I was not a priest?

As a child, I had had to be an obedient boy, and then an obedient priest. I knew what others expected of me and I knew my boundaries. I learned how to live in a fish bowl but I was not happy. Even though others around me were kind to me and very accommodating, they could sense I was not happy, but they didn't understand why ... nor did I ... some seemed content but I was not.

If you think for yourself and follow your own conscience, you're considered to be "stepping out of line." If you speak your own opinions out loud, you're considered a "dissenter." If you swim outside the group, you're considered "disloyal."

Those of us who have been in an abusive relationship can relate to the fish in the fishbowl story. Although there was an entire world outside of our own, we felt secure and safe swimming in our small circle. We would have been fearful of swimming outside our group. No one else seemed to be venturing forth ... and what if we couldn't get back into the group.

In thinking about venturing beyond the group boundaries you become a thinker, a dissenter, and you become politically dangerous, even though, in most other social contexts, dissent is seen as a sign of democracy and a challenge to change.

Having been a part of a self-righteous, patriarchal culture, I know that as an enabler in an addiction to power and control, I could justify my abusive thinking and actions to anyone, and because of my position, most would not question me.

Today, the media are helping us to have a voice, and parishioners who themselves may be living in abusive situations, are seeing the signs of abuse and are able to articulate their experience. They are saying "Enough!" And once you leave one abusive relationship, you are able to leave other abusive situations and addictions as well.

Many abused persons will be able to relate to the price I had to pay to get my freedom. I had invested a great deal of myself into my role as a priest—twenty-five years of my life! Upon leaving, I lost many contacts that I had had as a priest. I had to learn how to cope with the ensuing isolation and alienation, not only of leaving the priesthood but also of preparing myself to be known as a gay person.

It is said that an addiction will end only when the person reaches rock bottom. I learned how to feel helpless because I always thought that I had no choices in my life, although I did. This inability to make choices affected my self-esteem, perceptions, and behaviours.

Being unable "to see" the effect that the use of power and control, exercised by both my mother and the one percent, was having on me at the time, I felt trapped into a life of co-dependency, guilt, shame, fear, and perfectionism. Not having anyone to help me to see the situation I was in also contributed to my feeling helpless. Recovery requires a fundamental choice: addiction or wholeness.

Whatever the choices we have to make in our lives, they will probably involve some sort of "price" being paid. It was when I began to see the signs of my abuse that I understood what my body had been trying to tell me every time I became ill, about every five years.

Within the institution, I had everything I needed to live—housing, food, insurance, health benefits, a pension, resources of every kind, educational opportunities, access to professionals, and tips/stipends on the side. Three days after I was asked to leave, I lost all of those perks, except for my vehicle, which was my own.

For the abuse to end, and to never again allow myself to be subjected to it, I needed information about myself, and to have a language that would help me understand the situation I was in. I had learned to feel helpless and to feel constantly intimidated. I had acquired strong skills and abilities for survival and security, but my beliefs and values were those of others.

I began to see the impact that the institution was having on the ninety-nine percent, and in my case, upon my own parishioners. I began to dislike what I was asking of them, especially when I was beginning to no longer believe in what I was teaching, preaching and doing myself.

If you don't have family or friends who can help you financially, or if you haven't had the opportunity to save some money, you have a hurdle to get over. Your diocese may, out of a sense of justice, offer you some money to get you on your feet. But this "donation" will not be an unconditional gift. You might have to sign a waiver of silence in order to make sure you don't write about your experiences—another way of maintaining control over you, even when justice and compassion should be offered instead.

After years of what I perceived as abusive brainwashing, being treated like an object and having my focus of attention always on my abuser, being asked to leave provided a sense of freedom as I left the bishop's office for the last time. But still, to survive such a shock to my system, I needed to have a number of resources in place, or the shock would have immobilized me.

In seeking advice and counselling, I needed to understand the trauma of abuse and the psychological impact of having been abused; to feel that I was not being blamed, pathologized, judged, nor held responsible; to understand the difficulty of leaving and the societal sanctions against it; to understand my ambivalence and that I was not defined by my experience of abuse.

I could not have left without having my own apartment, another job, support from management, or emotional and psychological support from the staff. I could not have left without friends offering me empathy support, information, outside help, sensitivity, confidence, compassion, non-judgement, people to talk with, or without the re-education in clinical counselling that offered me a different perspective.

And I could not have left without outside help from medical, financial, legal and spiritual counselling.

The one percent maintains strong control over its co-dependent priests by making sure they have just enough money to exist. I was made to believe that I was at the service of the Church and God and, like Jesus, was to have no spare change. Have you ever seen how the one percent lives? It is nothing but the best for the men at the top, though I believe their lifestyle will change under Pope Francis.

Without the resources in place, I would not have been able to make the transition, and I would have subjected myself to a continuing abusive relationship. The one percent counts on us fearing for our security and having our self-doubt to prevent us from wanting to move on.

Luckily, the answers to all of my needs fell into place; otherwise the separation would have been even more traumatic because an abuser always enforces a separation by totally withdrawing compassion and further contact. But with all my needs being met in a fashion, the separation became freeing. Without that freedom, one remains abused, fearful, and in a constant state of vulnerability. It is only when I was given my freedom that I was able to see my life from a different perspective, and with hope.

I had lived a life of security and isolation under the control and brainwashing of an institution that I had always thought was going to be there for me, no matter what. My sexual behaviour was addictive because it had been a preoccupation and an obsession for me in order to maintain my denial of being in a condition of abuse. But my need for obsessive addictions was no longer needed, nor longed for, once I was empowered with freedom.

Of course, I continued to enjoy my sexual orientation and behaviour, but it was no longer obsessive. My personality and lifestyle required freedom but I had been trapped and powerless. Had I not been forced out of the system, I would have been submitted to being reprogrammed as an enabler, again, because I would have felt that I had no way out of the system, no choice but to stay.

Being of the Catholic Faith had always been very important to my parents. They never spoke of Christian Faith because for them the two were the same thing, the Catholic Faith being the "fullness" of the Christian Faith. For me, the Catholic Faith had nothing to do with having a good time, it was serious business and I was to take it seriously.

Our church was just down the street from our home, next to the parish school. The school was staffed by nuns and, in those days, all you could see were their hands and faces ... and the yardstick that seemed to grow out of one hand of the short little nun who was the principle. They taught us about our faith with religious instruction books called catechisms, which consisted of questions and answers.

One book prepared me for my first communion (Eucharist), another for my first confession, and another for my confirmation. Confirmation was like a public act of accepting Jesus Christ as my personal Lord and Saviour, though as Catholics we didn't say it that way. Today, with the "new evangelization" program, that pronouncement seems to be in vogue.

I was taught that as a Catholic, I possessed more of the truth and was more faithful to the teachings of Jesus. I believed that when Jesus died, the apostles began the Roman Catholic Church and from the time of St. Peter, the popes had continued to speak in the name of God himself.

I also believed that Mary was the mother of God, and the mother of the church. All these beliefs, rituals and practices that we Catholics had were understood as the "Will of God" being spoken through the church and, therefore, were to be obeyed without question.

Although there were many things I did not understand, I was told that I would understand them as I got older. I had so many questions about what I was being taught that didn't make sense to me, but I had to accept the teachings as "mysteries" of my faith that merely needed to be believed. I inherited my parents' faith, their form of worship, and their understanding of the truth as it had been taught to them. To question was somehow endangering my faith in God and my obedience to the church.

A big difference between me, and my Protestant friends seemed to be that they could read the Bible and I couldn't, though today it's being encouraged, thanks to the new evangelization program. Protestants also confessed directly to God but I couldn't. The new evangelization program hasn't changed that one.

As well, they were not on their knees as a family, praying to Mary for half an hour every day during the month of May, but I was. I felt sad that my friends were not going to the "One True Church instituted by Christ to give grace," as the catechism put it, and unless they converted to it, they could not go to Heaven, according to every Catholic adult in my Catholic world. But even as a child, I could not accept the idea that a loving God would agree with that kind of thinking, but to whom could I say such a thing? My parents would have been concerned for my faith and my immortal soul had they known what I was thinking.

Sunday in our home, with most of my friends still in bed because it was a holiday, was a Holy Day of obligation in Catholic homes. For my mother, trying to get us ready to go to church was a weekly ordeal, with her telling each of us what to wear and trying to stop us from complaining about having to go. We were well disposed for a prayerful experience.

Each week my parents had to separate us from each other in the church pew so we wouldn't cause a scene during Mass. They tried to keep us quiet during the sermon, and encouraged us to sing and respond to the prayers.

We had another family ritual that occurred every first Friday of the month—our fish and chips supper—and then we got ready for church again. I went along so as not to upset God and my parents, not because I enjoyed going.

Similarly, going to confession was the way that Catholics had of staying in God's good books. It was a mysterious irritant to me why we Catholics had to go into a dark, claustrophobic box called a confessional to tell our sins but my Protestant friends could speak directly to God

Each stage of preparation for these special "events" in our lives was made up of a series of definitions to be learned and a list of prayers to memorize. I had a lot of anxiety over not being ready to receive the rituals (sacraments). Imagine the humiliation of failing a religion course, somehow like failing God. Catechism was forming me to be a strong committed Catholic. It was an intellectual study of church doctrine and ritual preparations.

Some children had no "models" of religious faith because their parents were not involved in formal religion, though they were connected by tradition, as are many Christians. These parents were left with feelings of shame, resentment, guilt, and the hope that their children would be able to "get done" in a church.

"Getting done" was a preoccupation of most Catholic parents, who felt a guilt-ridden responsibility to make sure their children were baptized, received their first communion, their first confession, and then got confirmed, all before they left home.

After confirmation, I wondered what I had left to learn, despite the fact I knew almost nothing about the Bible or understood where it fit into all of the catechisms. My parents had a large gold edged Bible in our home. It had a visible place in the living room and had to be dusted periodically, along with the rest of the ornaments. My parents opened it to write in special family events, such as dates and details of births, baptisms, weddings and funerals.

As a child, I was discouraged from reading the Bible, being told that it was difficult to understand and that I might misinterpret it and be led astray. I didn't understand what all that meant but I did grasp that it could somehow be dangerous if I opened it and read it. Of course, that didn't make sense to me but I knew that if I read it and got confused or upset, then my parents would get upset themselves, and I would be threatened and made to fear their rejection. For me, nothing could be worse.

Those who shared and taught the Catholic Faith to me were well intentioned adults who were sincerely interested in teaching me the truth. But I was spiritually hungry at a very young age and had a lot of questions: What about the Bible that my friends studied? Why couldn't my Protestant friends go to Heaven? Why would a loving God want to punish these good people? What did people in other parts of the world believe in? Did Jesus become a Catholic before he died? I often felt frustrated and helpless in wanting my questions answered.

The rites of passage placed a tremendous burden on the pick-and-choose Catholics, which was lessened for those whose relatives were very generous contributors, or who were the pillars of the parish community, or who had a friend or relative who was a priest or deacon, or if the couple at least said that they would try to attend more regularly.

Mixed messages were being given. Some wanted only religious rituals, some wanted religious rituals and spirituality, and some searched for only spirituality. But the one percent, the men who made the decisions, didn't want changes, nor were they able to make any. Though the Roman Catholic Institution considers absolute obedience as loyalty, many people questioned what that had to do with what Christ came to teach. To the one percent, laws they make are the will of God and dictate what is right and what is wrong; what is God's way and what is sin.

These laws put added burdens—guilt, shame and resentment—on those who seldom attended worship, who wanted a divorce, who wanted to remarry, receive the sacraments, or have the opportunity to be listened to without judgment or condemnation.

Youth not only tend to reject the institution's sexual teachings but are also receptive to people who are not married both living together and having children, and they are more tolerant of freedom of sexual orientation.

My religious parents had offered their children a Catholic Faith foundation that they hoped we would also cherish. As a priest, I met many parents who found it very painful to see their children making different choices in the practise, or not, of their faith. Parents/guardians would ask themselves where they had gone wrong and if God would judge them for the choices their children made. They wondered if God would forgive their children, continue to bless them, and if one day God would let their children be with him in heaven?

Many believe that the only way they can be forgiven by God is by going to confession. Hence, many adults suffer emotionally over imaginary sins but don't confess them because they feel guilty about using the church for that purpose alone. And for many, the most pain comes from the guilt of denying their own feelings and beliefs. They live their lives as outcasts. They don't even ask God's forgiveness or pray to God because they interpret their relationship with God strictly according to the rules of the Catholic Institution and what they were taught as children in an era of blind obedience.

Most parents were given catechism (religious instruction) from books that consisted of questions and answers but today children are taught much differently and parents often feel poorly prepared, embarrassed, and threatened at their inability to express their faith to their children.

However, the majority of parents do have a very rich faith that comes from years of devotion to it. Many may have never shared their faith with their children in the way they share times of play, study, relaxation, and other forms of spiritual and quality time together.

In late 1992, the institution released its "New Catechism," the first since the Council of Trent in 1566. It was hailed by Pope John Paul II as one of the major events in the recent history of the Roman Catholic Church. Included as acceptable was birth control associated with self-discipline and infertile periods. Ordination was limited to baptized men, in keeping with Christ's own example but, still, the ordination of women was not possible.

Homosexuality was still against natural law but homosexuals should be treated with compassion and fairness, and be urged to be chaste. The "new evangelization" program and the conclusions of the 2012 Synod only repeat the statements made in 1992.

A new era is upon us in which people are no longer accepting control by guilt, shame, and intimidation. One of my bishops once wrote the following in our Catholic newsletter:

"If I were to call you a dissenter, a radical, leftist, agitator, individualist, activist, feminist or new pontificator; if I said you espouse a naïve version of liberation theology or moral relativism, that you spread disunity, confusion and evil in our midst, what would I accomplish? If you, in turn, called me orthodox, patriarchal, authoritarian, backward, stagnant, a papist, an abuser of authority, allowing others to do my thinking, what would you accomplish? You might answer that you speak in the name of justice, democracy and human dignity. I might say I speak with respect for the authority of God and His Word. Would we communicate? No! We would only hurt each other. And with every pain we inflict on each other, we make each other weaker, more vulnerable to attacks by others. Yet such "name calling" is frequent in our Church and in our archdiocese. Little wonder that the media exploit our weaknesses at every opportunity. Little wonder that unbridled Catholic "bashing" is now so commonplace. We bring it on ourselves."

Society has evolved, is more educated, less naïve, more tolerant, and though less religious, more spiritually conscious. And the one percent is about to be challenged by this society, which will not be tolerant of blind obedience and abuse of any kind, neither in the name of God, nor of motherhood.

Snapshots of my ministry

Seniors:
Seniors make up the core remnant in most Catholic churches today. Many young couples will be encouraged to participate more actively through the new evangelization

program, and youth will be listening attentively to what Pope Francis has to say to them that might encourage them to feel drawn to the church.

For many cultures, worship was just part of life, a part of the lives of all their relatives and family members. There was an unwritten expectation that one continued the traditions of the family. This was usually done with very good intentions but did not allow for individuality or the freedom to follow one's own conscience. When one went their own way, the rest of the family wondered what had gone wrong, and there was a very sincere concern for the wayward sheep, which was soon being referred to as the black sheep. Today, one looks around the church for any white sheep and sees mostly white-haired seniors.

Today, since fewer people are attending, they are encouraged to participate more in worship singing, to give more towards financial support, to participate more in the liturgy by doing the Sunday readings and helping to distribute communion, which, in their younger days to even touch the host (the consecrated bread) was wrong, but not quite a sin. Many see the involvement of the laity as taking over the priest's job, especially when it comes to hospital visitations. Seniors expect priests to be by the hospital bedside when they are sick, and especially when they are dying.

Many seniors are being open and understanding of the changes taking place. But for many, the changes cause much pain; any change in what is familiar can cause an upset. For some, when speaking of "spirituality," they think of the spiritual writings of the saints of the church, or of the devotional and ritual practices of the church.

Speaking of other kinds of spirituality has a "New Age" ring that causes them to take a cautious and suspicious stance.

They are well indoctrinated to believe that anything outside of the "official" stance of the one percent is to be avoided because it probably isn't of God. But seniors have years of wisdom on their side as well. They see what is happening in the church. And, as the regulations and demands of the one percent feel like a "heavy yoke" for them and their children, they are not as comfortable as they once were.

As I reflect back on the seniors in those parish communities where I served, and now see the situation of seniors in the church today, I understand why they are less comfortable because of the many changes that have taken place. At one time, they went to a service and just sat listening to a choir, and to the mystical Latin language. They could put two dollars in the collection plate without feeling guilty.

Women:

The participation of women involved going to ladies' group meetings and preparing for the Fall Supper. For the men, participation involved going to an Ushers or Knights of Columbus meeting. Both helped at fundraising functions and, of course, in getting their children done.

On the role of women within the life of the church the pope has said that "the church" (rather than saying the one percent) does not consider itself authorized to admit women to priestly ordination, although it recognizes the great importance of their participation in community life. Therefore, the ordination of women will never be a reality as long as the Roman Institution remains in its present addiction to power and control, and the one percent continues to justify, theologize, and canonize male celibacy.

I remember an archbishop being interviewed on television about his stance against women being ordained and against an active homosexual lifestyle. He said, " … if everyone disagrees with my position and that of the Church, then everyone is wrong."

It will take a man of this kind of arrogance and self-righteousness to keep the topics of women's ordination, married priests, and gays from ever becoming anything more than just topics of discussion among the ninety-nine percent. For the one percent, these topics remain non-issues … and priests are to remain silent on them.

What was the "place" of women in the feudal system? They were the maidens, the ladies of the court, the ladies in waiting. A woman attended to the needs of others. She was not in management but was always seen at the right had of whoever was in power.

In the current Roman feudal system, women will maintain their status as maidens in waiting. The idea of equality for women at the management level is totally unacceptable by the institution. Because of statements such as 1 Timothy 2: 11-12—"Women are to be silent" — women truly do have an uphill battle with the one percent, and although women today are ready for the fight, they are often tired of it.

Women are taught to be passive and form a culture of passivity among themselves, especially in the church.

Women are taught not to talk about things that are personal and how they feel about their role in the church. Being more aware of her own feelings, a woman is better trained to attend to the feelings of other people in an empathetic way. It is that sense of connection that will be so important within the new culture that is forming—contemplative, holistic, experiential, and open to the mystery of a personal God who is revealed in relationships. Female and gay male characteristics may explain why women far outnumber men at religious events and why gay men are attracted to the priesthood, and why the one percent tries to perpetuate a system of male, homophobic, celibate priests in the image of Jesus.

If women stopped contributing, both financially and actively, the one percent would quickly begin to sing a different tune. The institution continues to be viewed by many, as a sexist, patriarchal organization. Some women feel it is time for the institution to treat women with the same dignity it shows "straight" men.

Women's groups have been an organizational asset for all denominations, and yet in some denominations they have great difficulty finding congregations that want them as pastors. It has a lot to do with the traditional roles women have played in the institutions, and the sexism against women in society.

Aboriginal communities:
As with the aboriginal community I had just left, the people in all aboriginal communities are not preoccupied with church regulations. Problems of addictions and abuse were everywhere at the time and are still a major issue.

Families were divided by ties to other denominations, political struggles within the community, and by legal concerns and requirements. As in the south, young people were attracted to television ads and lifestyles.

Because of isolation, resources were limited and southerners would only stay for short periods of time. The people learned how to manipulate government resources and church paternalism. What was difficult to establish in the city parishes was even more difficult in the aboriginal communities because their beliefs, values, and needs were so different.

Domestic abuse was an unfortunate reality in most aboriginal communities. In the family, the victims of the abusive relationship between the parents were the children. Similarly, the victims of the abusive relationship between bishops and their priests were the parishioners.

Aboriginal communities struggled with the effects that residential schools had on them. Some were grateful for the education and support they received and needed to enter southern society. For others, the system was abusive. I could relate to their struggle because, as a priest, the church system had been an abusive experience for me whereas it was a fulfilling spiritual experience for other priests.

In order to maintain all the rules and regulations, the ninety-nine percent had to be convinced that obedience was a virtue and something for which they had to strive diligently. At the time of the patriarchal feudal system, it was not difficult to impose obedience upon the common people who knew no better, and who accepted their lot in life. In Catholic schools, homes, seminaries, convents and monasteries, we were taught to strive for obedience. There was always unrelenting pressure to "stay in line." There was little patience or compassion for human failings.

In the past, more so than today, if you disobeyed you were punished, often without an explanation, but this only developed anger and frustration. Rather than using forgiveness and compassion, those in authority seemed to prefer acts of cruelty and humiliation, and the punishment was always done "in the name of the Lord." Those who were subjected to residential schools attest to this.

Add this to the general humiliation and abuse that the aboriginal people were subjected to in being told their aboriginal beliefs and practices were not of God, and that they would have to leave their language, culture, customs, traditions, and spirituality if they wanted to be pleasing to God.

Those who abuse others have no idea of the humiliation and intimidation that their addiction to power and control has on those they abuse, which, for the aboriginal peoples of Canada, was all done in the name of the Lord.

Two additional factors added to their burden: the resurgence of their own spirituality and rituals when they were no longer considered illegal, and which called to their root experiences of their relationship with God; and the white culture's attempts to assimilate them.

Families were torn once again with some wanting to experience what they had been taught was pagan while fearing rejection by their more self-righteous family members who had come to believe that the old ways were truly pagan and not of God.

Some argued that you couldn't legislate morality, yet Catholics were taught that suicide was a serious sin. No one had the right to take his own life because it was a gift from God. When I became a priest, the one percent still showed little compassion for the loved ones left behind. Their laws stated that if you committed suicide, you could not be buried in a Catholic cemetery.

Therefore, those who committed suicide were buried on "the other side" of the fence, outside of the cemetery. Imagine the shame, guilt and pain of friends and relatives seeing their loved one being buried this way. This was just one case of where the law was a burden and an embarrassment.

As a priest, I met with many couples who had remarried, were going to church on special occasions, receiving the sacraments and were not worried about the "blessing" of the one percent. They would have been made to feel uncomfortable had they continued to attend on a regular basis. The institution no longer made them feel welcome. This was especially true among aboriginal people. Therefore, on special occasions, they would go to church with a free conscience before God and would not let the guilt of regulations stop them from experiencing a traditional ritual.

Churches at Christmas were always filled with people renewing this tradition and participating fully, whether the one percent liked it or not.

Young couples:

The one percent and its priests wanted to maintain control over the lives of their young couples because they were the financial base, and in the future, so would their children be. Young couples were forced to do things exactly the way the one percent wanted them done. Otherwise, the one percent would withhold the couples' need for a church wedding, and their future need to have their children "done." The one percent and their priests used the children as bargaining chips.

The behavioural effect that this abuse had upon these victims was that they withdrew from the institution when they did not need a rite of passage. They underachieved in that they did not use their talents, energy and vision for the service of the institution. They refused to get involved and to support the institution in its directives and regulations. They felt aggression in what was asked of them and responded by becoming passive. They became defensive by being aloof.

Many accepted that God created us to be passionate sexual beings. However, Catholics are constantly plagued with guilt when it comes to the topic of sexuality. We were taught that sacrifice, suffering, and abstinence are the true way to redemption, and that the clerics are present to remind us of our sinfulness, the abuse of our bodies, our disobedience and humanity. And all this, for the most part, comes from old, celibate, asexual, patriarchal, clerical men who believe that masturbation and premarital sex are serious sins.

People may want and need many of the rites and traditions but the one percent controls them by keeping a tight rein on who is deemed to be worthy. People must prove their intentions to them ... so much for Jesus' movement of wanting to "set people free." They institutionalized his movement and have placed a "heavy yoke" upon young couples.

Subconsciously, I felt that this was what was happening to me, but I didn't fully recognize it. I had projected upon the young people my feelings of anger and frustration at the trivial demands of the one percent, demands that had nothing to do with the freedom that Jesus had come to bring us. I was angry at the one percent, not the church.

The result was that such couples refused to live within the stifling, degrading, humiliating, and demanding limitations of the institution. As with so many young couples, they continued to be forced to endure living in a cycle of "picking and choosing" their needs while the one percent and their priests lost all their credibility.

With our Higher Power

*M*any Christian groups have equated religiosity and God and have "personified" God by saying things like, God says … God is deeply saddened by … or He has calmly backed out. A loved one dies and we say, "God knows best."

We personify God to justify our self-righteous desires to speak out about our concerns, such as the fact many do not want prayers in schools, many do not read the Bible, parents and teachers don't discipline children properly, some women have abortions, couples use condoms, the entertainment industry promotes profanity, violence and illicit sex, people too easily trash God, and public discussion of God is suppressed.

Concerning religion, some say it's only a matter of time until things rebound. Others speak of a pendulum-like swing. Some believe that religion is unlikely to be replaced by secular substitutes. Some believe that new religious groups will arise in response to the core questions of existence, death, tragedy, obligation and love. Some believe that this accounts for the emergence of charismatic and evangelical groups.

Also, trying to help us understand the meaning of life is the New Age Movement, which is often spoken about along with other "fringe" activities like meditation, astrology, tarot cards, reincarnation, out-of-body experiences, and dream analysis.

However, the New Age Movement has become a significant spiritual movement. It has focused on the tapping of one's potential, personal spirituality, the spirit world, the oneness of creation, the limitless potential of humanity, and possibility of transforming the self and today's world into a better one.

That the one percent is so fearful and defensive about the New Age Movement is understandable. It threatens the status quo and the income of orthodox religious groups and cannot be contained in a "box." It is often spoken of out of fear, self-righteousness, lack of tolerance, and insecurity.

With these attitudes of denial, minimizing, justifying, rationalizing, and blaming from those addicted to power and control, many among the ninety-nine percent and the clerical subculture are saying, "Enough!" As people move on in their social, political, economic and cultural lives, they also move on in their spiritual lives. They leave behind the politics of denominational concerns about membership, dogma, and self-righteousness.

Change often puts things into perspective and cleanses the soul. People are at peace with their educated consciences as they search for forms and expressions of spirituality that connect their lives more closely within themselves, with others, and with God.

Many are searching for forms and expressions of spirituality that will enable them to articulate their personal experience and help them connect their lives more closely. For some, that will mean joining another denomination or religion. For others, it will mean supplementing their present faith experience with New Age spirituality, creation spirituality, or native spirituality.

It is known that the world can "articulate" itself through the body. This notion can help to explain what is sometimes called "the sixth sense" or the ability to acquire knowledge about a person or an event without the use of the ordinary means of perception. It seems to imply some kind of underlying unity in creation whereby particular items of information can occasionally be deciphered by people with the right kind of psychic sensitivity. Psychologists refer to this as "clairvoyance," ascetical theology talks of "infused knowledge," and Hinduism refers to "subtle consciousness."

Our sexuality, far from being a distraction from God, can be understood as the instrument by which God created us, and through which he continues to manifest himself to us. People are blinded to the holiness of the flesh by guilt, shame and fear put on them by the one percent. A "gay" spirituality is necessarily sex positive. Sex is God's gift of love and being loved by another is a way of experiencing God's love for us.

Gay people represent the exuberance for fun, pleasure, playfulness, imagination and creativity. Our identity is in relationships. In gay relationships, sex is God's love through us. We need to feel loved. We need to be touched in order to grow and to stay healthy and vibrant. Jeffrey P. Dennis, in the magazine *The Other Side*, September, 1993, wrote an article entitled, "Liberating Gay Theology" in which he says: "We need a gay God, a God who would lead us toward a more affirming, harmonious and creative, socially conscious, and spiritually profound life."

Sounds like the message of Jesus, except for the gay God part. And Toby Johnson, in *Gay Spirituality*, writes: "As gay people, we have to create our own explanations, our own myths, our own visions of why God created us this way and what it means to be homosexual."

I know what it feels like to go through experiences without a language to express feelings and emotions; to be treated as an object, programmed to obey and not to question; to be labelled as disobedient and yet know that you're a good person who has the respect and love of others, and of God. To be made to feel guilty for not fitting in, for wanting to do your own thing, and hurting the others around you who want you to be accepted by the institution, and in turn, by God.

This wholeness of vision was seen in Jesus. This prophet and visionary came for people of all faiths and spiritualties, not to convince them to change their faith, but to live it out in a more harmonious and healthy way. He came to give the spirituality (not a religion) that we are looking for today and that he tried to bring to us 2000 years ago through " ...loving God with all our being, and our neighbour as ourselves."

But, alas, Christian groups have had difficulty putting the three themes of "God, self and society" together.

The outline of the in-service I mentioned a long way back in this book said that God has called us "to be" healthy, and we are healthy when we are in harmony within ourselves, in relationship with our bodies, minds and spirit. We are in health when there is harmony in our relationships between ourselves and in our relationship with our higher power.

The prophet Jesus said the same thing 2000 years ago and, unfortunately for him and us, his followers turned his vision into another religion and, by making it into an institution, lost that vision.

Jesus did not speak the language of laws but of love … a love that gets deeply involved with the joy and pain of living.

Jesus, in asking us to "love God with our whole heart, mind and soul, and our neighbour as ourselves," was saying that we have to be able to love ourselves before we can love anyone else. And in loving our neighbour, we show our love of God by being in healthy relationships, which he created us to be in. By loving this way, we, in turn, consciously live out his vision of bringing the Kingdom of God to our social context. And by living this out one day at a time, we will be in harmony within ourselves, between ourselves, and with our Higher Power.

There is no place for self-righteous claims on the "truth" in today's multicultural world. Even when religious groups stick to religion, they may not have a lot of freedom to be very assertive. Academics have legitimized the "everything is relative" idea. Religious groups are called upon to recognize that ours is now a multi-faith world. The principles of tolerance and acceptance are the norm. There is little room or appreciation for competition. If a variety of lifestyles, moralities, and religions are all to have a place under one societal roof, each must be seen as a valid option for all.

Truth has to be seen in terms of personal preference. A society that is multicultural cannot permit proponents of one cultural style or sexual orientation, abortion view or world view to impose its positions, its "truths" on others. The diplomatic way to resolve the problem of diverse outlooks is to decree that they all are relative.

I have moved beyond the religiosity of the denomination that I lived in and served for most of my life, with its dogmas, expectations and rituals. I left, not with anger, but with disappointment, and a profound feeling of freedom.

I respect those who continue to find fulfillment and spiritual support in their particular denomination, along with a profound feeling of freedom. I respect the ministers who serve their communities with devotion, respect, and a sense of mission and vision.

My writing comes from the years of experience I have had at being abused, both as a child and as a tamed adult, and from having been able to move on. Once I experienced freedom, my behaviour changed and the regime could no longer control me. Without its expectations on me, I can live with hope. And it is my hope that my spiritual journey will help others to discover what they need to learn to continue, or to move on with their own spiritual journeys in a different direction.

I hold this hope especially for women who hope for equality within the Catholic institution; gay priests who hope for acceptance; all women and men who are being abused in their relationships; all who get tears in their eyes when they speak of the pain that the Catholic Institution has caused them; all who want to move on but are filled with so much guilt and fear; all who want to live deeper spiritual lives in their religious faith; and all who are searching for something spiritual that can be meaningful and fulfilling for them.

Each person has been created to fulfill a unique role in creation; discovering that role and living it out is what counts, not how it compares to others.

Concerning the 'New Evangelization' Program

*R*egulations are a powerful form of intimidation—our Catholic "dos and don'ts." In my day, the institution would often introduce them as, "The Church's official position is …"

However, it would have been more accurate to introduce them as "The hierarchy's official position is …"

When the statements were proclaimed, some argued about them, priests had to try to defend them, and some tried to convince themselves that the institution was only human after all. Some claimed that the institution was enriched with a heritage and tradition that came down from St. Peter himself, and others believed that these traditions were handed down to us directly by Jesus.

The issue of annulments was a case in which the law was a burden and an embarrassment in the fact that they were the only way to remarry with the church's blessing. But the issue was disciplinary not doctrinal.

The institution was pushed into a solution or loose vast numbers of paying customers whose marriage was over but who often wanted to stay loyal to the church.

The Eastern Orthodox Church, which separated from Rome in 1054, forgave one marital mistake and gave people a second chance. The Roman institution, however, insisted on annulments. People saw no way out so many would yield to the accompanying package of rules and regulations—to the power and authority of the one percent—in order to remarry with the institution's blessing.

The church fathers that met for the October, 2012, Synod in Rome were all surprised at the influence of secularization and similar challenges around the world. Many of the fathers saw secularization negatively, as people not wanting to hear about Christian values and wanting same-sex marriage. Yet they realized the terms "secularization" and "consumerism" might have been over stressed in the past.

Finding themselves limited by pastoral frustrations, some voiced the need to "look at the heart" of people before looking at how they behave. They don't know how to respond to the life of the people and are beginning to see, fifty years after the Second Vatican Council that they have not been diligent enough in considering what it is people are actually looking for.

This entire book is an attempt to explain my experience as an illustration of why the one percent will always be unable to see what people are looking for—because the one percent looks at people through the tinted glasses of power and control! These men in pointed hats are not able to respect and revere the new spiritual language while wearing those glasses. It is a language largely spoken outside of religious institutions, yet does not have the intention of excluding them.

The one percent sees this language of emerging spiritualties as self-preoccupation, or as giving glory to oneself, which, by the way, is where the prophet Jesus asked us to start. The fathers maintain the medieval language of referring to Jesus as humble and as having shown us the face of God the Father as one who loves by emptying himself. But that same Jesus also loved the "outsiders," those who, today, still remain voiceless in the Catholic Institution: women, the divorced, gays, and those of other faiths and spiritualties.

At the same time that some of the fathers might be saying they need a new impulse, vision, and spirit, they are now going to be stressing the exact point that was intended by the council fifty years ago, and in the words of Pope John XXIII: "It is not that the Gospel has changed; it is that we have begun to understand it better … The moment has come to discern the signs of the times, to seize the opportunity and to look far ahead."

Fifty years later, the Catholic Church has decided that it needs to define what is meant by "new evangelization" and "to look back" at 1962 and the Second Vatican Council. Members of the one percent feel they need to look at the "search" and the "new wisdom" that has come up.

The problem for them is that the language is outside of their vision of the "one holy Catholic Church." They have lost two generations of church goers. The new Catholics are second and third generation and need a new sense of identity through an ongoing formation, hence, the need for an informed laity for evangelization.

While the Catholic Church sat back watching its numbers decline, other Christian denominations centred their teachings, not on doctrines and regulations, but on building communities focussed on bringing people to a personal relationship with Jesus Christ, which, for many Catholics, is an uncomfortable language because, until now, it has been labelled Protestant.

The Catholic Church, in experiencing a crisis of faith, is now using a language with expressions such as "a personal relationship with Jesus Christ" and living "an abundant life" that it has not used during the past fifty years. It is a language that other emerging Christian communities have been using.

For those who have remained in the pews, the new evangelism that will be introduced to all Catholics will make many feel very uncomfortable, the majority of whom have been going to church faithfully for Sunday Mass throughout the crisis of faith, which was brought on by scandals unrelated to them.

The Catholic tradition of, and reverence for Mary as the mother of the church, and the practice of reciting the rosary are foreign to the modern secular generation and the non-Catholic Christian community that speaks a different spiritual language, and which has little tolerance for self-righteousness and dogma.

Vision:

To be creative, you need a safe environment in which to share your vision. In today's environment, it is not safe to speak of married or gay clergy and women priests because the system has to defend its power and control, and uses silencing to ensure obedience and faithfulness. If priests are disloyal to the Roman Catholic Institution, public shaming and condemnations are used to ensure orthodoxy.

Youths today feel "called" to develop consciences that can lead them far beyond a world of no drugs and no premarital sex to a vision, a "call" for a compassionate church, ready to bridge the gaps of poverty, abuse of power, and the role of women in the church on the one hand, and away from self-righteousness and institutionalization on the other.

Those who are visionary, contradictory, not seen as part of the group, are looked upon as rebels, as making waves, and are not considered to be positive contributors. However, they are considered as not content in working within the system and trying to make improvements from within. They are seen as displeased and dissatisfied, terms that explain them away and, therefore, they can be asked to capitulate or move on.

In church teachings, dissent is unacceptable. Criticism is seen as disloyal but it is difficult for many to settle into a rigid, conforming system, just as it is for an abused partner to merely acquiesce. Even the thought of doing things differently, of needing a fundamental restructuring affecting the one percent is frightening and threatening, especially for those who are among those addicted to the current system of power and control.

Pope Benedict's resignation came with shock from those with him as he made his announcement, and with suspicion from those outside Vatican walls. But the one percent was quick to support him by referring to him as a simple, gentle, humble, courageous, even heroic man who felt that this era required a healthier, more vibrant pope to better handle the burden of Atlantic travel.

Many of us outside the Vatican continue to have our own theories. During his last week in office, Pope Benedict made use of his private audiences to speak against what he referred to as "the dictatorship of relativism." And what is relativism?

"Teaching morality doesn't mean imposing my moral values on others. It means sharing wisdom, giving reasons for believing as I do … and then trusting others to think and judge for themselves.[1]" With this definition, it is not difficult to see why Pope Benedict would "fear" such a subjective understanding of freely choosing according to ones' own conscience.

As I have been saying, the one percent feels that it is their divine right to tell us what God wants us to believe and do, and they do so in the name of the Church of Jesus, whether you're a Catholic or of another spiritual faith.

In the same papal audience of February 13, 2013, Pope Benedict also stated: "We can't exist without God," and on that point I totally agree, though my understanding and personal relationship with my God is different.

He went on to say, "We need religion to be connected to history." Again, I agree to a point, but this is not the case at this time in our human spiritual evolution. He also said, "We need faith and reason as the pillars of our existence." But which faith, and which educated "reason?"

---

[1]   …See for example: www.moral-relativism.com

I suspect that he was referring to both as those taught by the Catholic Institution.

Then, when he addressed the priests of Rome on February 14, 2013, what I found very telling was that after his talk, half the priests applauded and the others didn't. He referred to the "council of the fathers" and the "council of the media."

I found the facial expression of many of the priests on hearing that to be quite telling.

If the media reveals or challenges the statements from the one percent, the media is perceived as it has always been in the past, as engaging in "church bashing," presumably in a fashion similar to the "gay bashing" engaged in by the one percent for their own purposes.

In the same audience that day, the pope went on to say that "Our task is church renewal and true renewal is with the council Fathers"—a sentiment I am certain is not shared by other Christian faith communities.

In some countries, the separation of church and state means having a state that does not recognize God or religion at all. A positive lay state keeps church and state separate but recognizes God, or a Higher Power, in its laws and structure. This language is very uncomfortable for the one percent, who sees any loss of power and control as a personal attack on them and, in turn, upon God himself.

The tolerance of "religious freedom" in Russia today puts the Catholic Church in a delicate situation in which it feels it needs to be present and vocal and yet needs to be very sensitive to the reality that it is a minority faith and that the major Christian faith in Russia is the Orthodox Church. But the Catholic Church is not comfortable in second position, nor is it tolerant and respectful of other faith communities in which it is not the major Christian denomination. I often experienced that phenomenon as a Catholic priest in northern aboriginal communities in which there were several Christian churches, all bidding for the souls within those small settlements, which resulted in family divisions and resentments.

Pope John XXIII had a unique vision of grassroots renewal of the church. The problem is that no one else shared nor understood his vision. He was surrounded by the one percent wearing tinted glasses, and his successor interpreted his vision by introducing the "Collegiality of Bishops," which only strengthened the bond and fraternity of the one percent but did nothing for that grassroots vision. We will now witness a new effort by the one percent to respond to its crisis of faith in introducing a very worthwhile new evangelization, which has already been in practice by non-Catholic Christians for the past fifty years.

Included in this new evangelization will be an attempt to awaken in the ninety-nine percent an appreciation of the Bible and using the Scriptures in their daily lives. They quote St. Jerome as having said that an ignorance of the Word is ignorance of Jesus. Where was this wisdom when we were discouraged from reading the Bible back in the 50s and earlier?

The one percent is trying to make it very clear that they see Scripture as very important. They did show their interest back in 1980 they supported the interim steering committee's efforts to establish the first Catholic Bible College, in Canmore, British Columbia.

But in the end, all the efforts put into the realization of that college evaporated. At the time, I couldn't understand why the hierarchy could let something like that happen when there was such an interest and support. The power and control that the hierarchy had upon everything we wanted to do had a profound effect on me. Everything had been going along so well. The laity had spent years and many hours doing all the ground work: research, reports, studying with sub-committees throughout their provinces, meeting with bishops and finance committees, finding a suitable building, and hiring a director from applicants across Canada.

Now, with the language and understanding of abuse, I understand what was happening, and why it ended the way it did. The hierarchy allowed representatives from the ninety-nine percent, and the clergy, to do the work, but the one percent needed to make it clear to everyone that they were in charge. But the Bible College was to be based on grassroots support—support and the control of the ninety-nine percent—and when that was taken from them, the vision was lost and the structure came apart.

Once again, the one percent let it be known that it would be their way or no way. At the time, I didn't understand what had happened. Years later, I returned to Canmore to see what was left. I met someone taking care of the property and asked him what happened and he simply said that the bishops had made their presence felt.

Youth:
Not much has changed for young people in the institution in the last twenty-five years. Although I am able to

better articulate the experience I had with the youth, my observations and insights have not changed. Young people are powerless and vulnerable before the one percent. Many see themselves as "committed" and attend services on a weekly basis, often following in parental footsteps. Although many have no religious preference, they are influenced by their religious culture when the need for the "rites of passage" comes along.

In terms of what is important to them, they tend to rank the search for truth, harmony with nature, spirituality, and an interest in religious involvement in that order. They believe they have spiritual needs and how they live will influence what happens to them after they die. Their fascination with supernatural phenomena exceeds that of older generations and they give some credibility to just about everything.

Young people are searching. Many leave not only their denominations but also their "religion." They have a void or a gap, an emptiness, and they do not know which way to turn. Often they lose faith and hope and go into themselves with drugs.

One day, when they need the rites of passage, or to have their own children done, these young "rebels" will experience the wrath of the one percent and many of its lackey priests. They will, perhaps, go to a Catholic youth rally with these priests who enable the one percent, and they will be hurt and angry. At the rally they will cry, laugh, sing and celebrate with the priests, but when they come face to face with them later, the one percent will look at them from their throne of power and humiliate, degrade, blame, judge, label, and self-righteously withhold their support from them, because these young people did not do as the church had wanted them to do. They will say to the young people, "Our way or the highway," and they will say it to them with little compassion, little respect, and no understanding.

Today, even more so than when I was a young priest, the youth of the world is going beyond religiosity and the institution's understanding of right and wrong. Many young Catholics approve of safe premarital sex when love is involved, and many are currently sexually involved. Many approve of homosexual relationships. Many feel that a legal abortion should be possible when rape is involved, and many feel it should be possible for any reason, as part of a woman's right to control her own God-given body.

For the one percent and the priests to tell young people to be "good kids," not have sex, and that they are the future of the church is not meeting the needs of those young people. The paternalistic institution is trying to speak to a generation that has different views and terms of reference—a different language.

For the most part, young people have a very sincere love and respect for the pope, they enjoy being with him, they recognize him as a holy man, but he is simply not speaking their language, which involves self-awareness, basic needs, and ways of expression.

I know what it feels like to go through experiences but not have a language to express one's feelings and emotions; to be treated like an object, programmed to obey and not to question; to be labelled as disobedient, and yet know that you're a good person that has a respect and love of others and of God; to be made to feel guilty for not fitting in, for wanting to do your own thing, and in the process hurting others around you who want you to be accepted by the institution and, in turn, by God.

Twenty-five years after entering the priesthood, having acquired a language for my experiences, I understand the experiences that the youth of our day share with believers and non-believers alike in having a thirst for truth, a hunger for solidarity, and a desire for self-giving. But the abusive institution, as in any abusive home, cannot offer the freedom that respect and understanding require.

Media:

Once again, it took the media to expose another part of the shadow side of the one percent. The one percent minimizes uncomfortable situations by representing events, such as the pedophile scandals, as being less serious that they actually are in order to protect their clerics from facing criminal charges, which any one of the ninety-nine percent would have to do in the same circumstances. To add insult and pain to this injustice of harbouring criminals and protecting sexually abusive priests, they silence everyone involved.

Finally, in having its own treatment centres, the one percent has been able to police its members and enablers and to use psychiatrists to put their pedophile priests back into circulation.

Having been a part of a self-righteous patriarchal culture, I know that as an enabler within an addiction of power and control, I could justify my own abusive thinking and actions to anyone, and because of my position, most would not question me. Today, the media are helping us have a voice, and parishioners, who themselves may be living in abusive situations, are seeing the signs of abuse and are able to articulate their experience, and boldly say, "Enough!"

The need for mutual respect:

Since the mid-1990s, Russia has gone from a systematic atheism to a pragmatic atheism. Generations of individuals have grown up in Russia either hiding their spirituality in their private families or submitting to the propaganda of a systemic atheism.

Since Pope John Paul II, there has been an openness to the Catholic Church into a predominately Orthodox population, which has received a renewed government acceptance since the twentieth century in which many of its older citizens have met the return of the Catholic Church with mistrust and suspicion.

The Catholic Church realizes that it must not try to be overpowering and must be very respectful of the Orthodox tradition that is entrenched in the Russian culture. Both the Orthodox and Catholic spiritualties share a common belief in their faith in Christ and in the sacraments, and share many values that both traditions defend: the right of religious freedom, the family, and the unborn.

The Catholic Church, with its more modern and open-minded educational resources, offers Russians centres for dialogue and mutual respect to all those searching for the meaning of faith, of God, and of Christ, while not overpowering the Orthodox majority. It is a much-needed service because there is a lack of a language in Russia with which to articulate one's faith and concepts of spirituality, such as God and the meaning of life.

As in previous generations, Catholics go to church to receive the sacraments, be forgiven, and to be buried, but don't ask a Catholic to explain what it is all about. I know that when I was a child and my Protestant friends would ask me something about my Catholic Faith I could always resort to my usual answer: "It's a mystery." That line won't work today with our educated and not so naïve society, which won't accept " …because the church says so" as a satisfactory answer for anything, even in Russia.

The Orthodox and Catholic Churches are faced with similar concerns and can work together as a united front in facing the issues of their youth and young families, those of secularism and atheism, and of the growing Muslim presence, of which both are fearful rather than respectful. The Catholic Church is hoping its spiritual brothers in the Orthodox Faith will be like them. But the Catholic Church will not be able to impose its papal authority on others of faith, whether they share the same faith of not.

In the western world, the Catholic Church has much to be witness to; not only the freedom of religion, which includes those of other religions, but also today's society that has evolved into one of freedom of conscience, freedom of choice, inclusivity, and tolerance toward everyone's choice of spiritual and sexual expression. Until the Catholic Church can respect and revere individual freedom, it will not be able to speak in a language that is used by society and, especially, by its youth. It will only be a matter of time when those in secular society, many of whom have become very spiritual though not religious, will find the self-righteousness and arrogance of the one percent unacceptable and irrelevant to their spiritual growth and relationship with God.

The one percent has marginalized and minimized many exceptional theologians, one of whom was Henri Nouwen, a Dutch-born Catholic priest who was a university professor and who authored forty books. He lived from 1932-1996 and was buried near Daybreak in the Sacred Heart Cemetery in Toronto, Ontario.

And few Roman Catholic theologians have received the wide recognition in the twentieth century among Christians of all kinds that Hans Kung, born in Sursee, Switzerland, March 19, 1928, has.

Kung's prolific writings questioned the formulation of such traditional church doctrine as papal infallibility, the divinity of Christ, and teachings about the Virgin Mary.

In 1979, a Vatican censure that banned his teaching as a Catholic theologian provoked international controversy and, in 1980, a settlement was reached at Tubingen that allowed him to teach under secular rather than Catholic auspices.

In *The Guardian* of October 27, 2009, an article written by Hans Kung, "The Vatican Thirst for Power Divides Christianity and Damages Catholicism,[2]" from which this extract has been taken.

Just as we have seen over many centuries – in the east-west schism of the eleventh century, in the sixteenth century Reformation, and in the First Vatican Council of

---

[2] See for example: www.theguardian.com/profile/hans-kung

the nineteenth century – the Roman thirst for power divides Christianity and damages its own church. It is a tragedy.

Then, "Hans Kung's open letter to Catholic Bishops,[3]" was posted on May 3, 2010 in *Independent Catholic News* and from which these brief excerpts have been taken.

Missed is the opportunity to make the spirit of the Second Vatican Council the compass for the whole Catholic Church, including the Vatican itself, and thus to promote the needed reforms in the church … I want only to lay before you six proposals that I am convinced are supported by millions of Catholics who have no voice in the current situation. … 1. Do not keep silent: By keeping silent in the face of so many serious grievances, you taint yourselves with guilt. When you feel that certain laws, directives and measures are counterproductive, you should say this in public. Send Rome not professions of your devotion, but rather calls for reform!

When the youth gathered with the Pope:

In 1984, when Pope John Paul II came to Canada and met with young people, I wrote that when the youth gather with the pope, they are waiting for a father's words on the meaning of life. The pope encouraged them to have the courage to commit themselves to the truth, to the fullness of life found in Jesus, and to the love God has for each of his sons and daughters. He reminded them that personal tragedies require acts of love and solidarity toward those who are lost or suffering. Love for life and the moral norms for living according to God's design

---

[3] See for example: http://www.indcatholicnews.com/news.php?viewStory=15996

do not comprise a theory to be learned from a book but written in the hearts, minds and consciences of all.

In many modern societies, consciences are ignored or deformed. Some say that the gatherings of the youth with the pope give a greater appreciation of the pope, of his own person, but also of his teaching, and also an appreciation of the universal character of the church.

However, the next time you're in a church service, look around; look for the youth. Even many of those who attend youth rallies for the pope won't be found in church. They are very sincere in wanting to see the pope and to hear him speak. They are sincere in wanting to meet other young Catholics like themselves. So why aren't they in church?

The young people today are responding as would any abused child who is part of a victimized group. When they are in the church community they feel stifled, ignored and manipulated. They know that if they don't go along with the desires of their parents, life will be tense. They know that if they don't attend religious studies they will not get "done," and they know what the emotional consequences of that will be.

So, what do they do? They do what any abused child would do. They act out, they withdraw, they become passive, aloof, sarcastic, and very open minded. They cannot say to the one percent and to priests what they think, or speak of what they want because they know what will happen. So they wait patiently for the day when they are on their own, and then they, too, will be forced to enter into the cycle of getting done.

Young people want to love the one percent and their priests, but they are unable to because they are being treated like disobedient children who, unless they do as they are told and behave the way the one percent wants them to, they will not have their needs met and support will be withheld. The one percent, and many priests, expect and demand that the youth go to church on Sundays, follow the rules and regulations of the institution, and do so silently and reverently.

Fast forward to the 2013 "Catholic Olympics" as some media referred to the World Youth Days held on the Copacabana Beach in Rio de Janeiro or, as the Cardinal of NYC put it: "During Mardi Gras, a place of Sodom and Gomorrah, but now turned into a time of joy, faith and solidarity."

The $60-million Catholic spectacle included incense during all rituals: the mass, adoration of the blessed sacrament, vigils, the angelus, the way of the cross, the Lord's prayer sung in Latin, with priests in cassocks, thousands of volunteers and security, and hundreds of thousands of youth from around the world immersed in talks called catechesis. "Catechesis" means an education in the faith, with a view to initiating the hearers into the fullness of Christian (Catholic) life.

The catechesis sessions were one of the principle activities of World Youth Days, taking place in churches, schools, arenas, and other venues throughout the vast city of Rio. The same script was followed everywhere, with three main themes: hope, discipleship and mission.

The one percent was in full form, even if they were physically tested. For me, the tone was set when the

Cardinal, speaking to the English youth, started referring to an image that I'm sure most of them never saw, of "the Sacred heart of Jesus," which, as a child, I was very familiar with. Then the speaker said that "Our hearts are longing, searching for Jesus, and Jesus has provided everything in the church. For Catholics, Jesus and the church are one."

Having gone to Rio as pilgrims, another cardinal reminded the young crowd that St. James, as the patron of pilgrims, "saw his martyrdom as a fulfillment, the 'logic' of the journey, the image of God that calls us on a journey, the great journey of dislocation. He spoke of the saints as models and Mary as the integral part of the Catholic faith, the mother of those going to Jesus and the first one to follow him."

Another cardinal told them that discipleship is costly … to our very lives, but implored them not to be afraid, but instead to be counter-cultural because many others had lost their lives as martyrs, and said young people need to be missionaries in their schools and on the Internet.

Francis did his part by telling them that they are leading history forward and not to let anyone take away their hope, even if their parents are not good models. He told them to listen to their grandparents (those still left in church) who are passing on their religious heritage and transmitting the wisdom of their lives.

At one of the catechism sessions, a young person put a very poignant and revealing question to the speaker when he asked: "How do you juggle between being a friar and a cardinal?" The dear cardinal didn't see that one coming and his reaction and response were both very awkward.

Another youth said, "We are only youth and don't have the skills to speak in apologetics," to which it was suggested, "Study your faith."

Apologetics is a branch of theology concerned with the defence of, or proof of Christianity ... in this case, of Catholic Christianity.

The same friar then, referring to the Gospel of St. John, said that Jesus spoke of the "new commandment," which I hadn't realized was another of Jesus' commandments, by saying, "They will know me (Jesus) by your love for each other." And after the commandment, he gave them a gift, the Eucharist, to "Do this in memory of me."

Then the friar told them, "We need a game plan" in order to continue. His "game plan" was for them to receive the Eucharist and pray daily in order to hear the living voice of Jesus in prayer, especially in silence before the Blessed Sacrament.

Imagine what it must have been like for many of those young people—still in their studies, in the process of educating their own free consciences, immersed in a secular world, evolving in a society of relativism and consumerism, with little religious experience because most of their parents had stopped being regular church attenders—hearing from celibate, patriarchal men that Jesus and his church are relying on them to go to the front lines and bring back the lost.

Francis spoke of a "culture of encounter" in which a constructive dialogue is the only way to grow. Shortly after, he told the media that the topic of women ordination was a closed issue, and to the same media he said, in effect: "Who am I to judge a gay person if they are on a journey to God?"

He continued a mantra that would be echoed continually: that the Lord is asking the youth to follow him in his (Catholic) church. He tells them they are, in an orderly way, to be "protagonists" to build a better world. I would like to add that gay priests tried that but were quickly silenced.

Little wonder that one of the cardinals found solace in Benedict's "Dictatorship of relativism" quote when judging people like me when we say that we are spiritual but not religious. In his words, we are frauds because he believes that Jesus came and died so we could have community and support and be a part of a community that speaks the same language. But many have found community and support in spiritual communities that are not religious, and in spiritual communities that speak the same language.

But that cardinal, while wearing tinted glasses formed out of his addiction to power and control, and believing that one has to be religious in order to be spiritual, will continue to justify his arrogant self-righteousness in judging others as fraudulent and pagan. For enablers to try to dialogue with the one percent is often an abusive experience and an exercise in apologetics, which is futile and unnecessary.

North America was referred to as being secularized. The word "secularize" can be defined as being separate from religious or spiritual connection or influence … to make worldly or unspiritual, or to imbue with secularism.

With this definition, North America doesn't stand alone, but I contend that it is in this cultural reality that educated, free individuals can choose a spirituality, whether religious or not, that will guide them in their search for a power higher than themselves.

One of the cardinals said that today it's trendy to say that one is a "New-Age atheist" without faith, and yet have hope. He went on to say that he calls the "ultimate hope" God. On that, I am in total agreement, although for me, God is Divine Energy and not "Father."

The youth were then told that it's in this secularized culture that their faith is distorted by the media, such as when the church is criticized for its position on "sanctity of life." It's the role of the media, however biased, to report issues and not to report them as dogmatic certitude, whether the subjects of a particular story believe their stance to be infallible or not.

We, fortunately, do live in a democracy with freedom of speech and lifestyle. Granted in the medieval era when the Catholic Church had political power as well, and dictatorships were the norm, it was a much more comfortable and influential time for an institution addicted to power and control. But those days are over and we have evolved. Fortunately, in North America and in many countries of the world, there is a separation between church and state.

To the young people whose consciences are still forming and who are still discerning careers and relationships, not to mention their own spiritual journey, Francis said that while we are quick to help those who are materially in need, we need not be indifferent to those who are spiritually in need ... many of whom are among the one percent, I might add.

He asked them to help street people and to defend life. He reminded them of the importance of marriage in order to pass on the Catholic faith, because the family is the "core" of the Catholic Faith.

He also asked them to overcome secularization by rejecting cultural trends that take them away from the Gospel. He asked them to be missionary disciples of the new evangelization and, again, reminded them that Jesus and the church and himself, the pope, are counting on them.

Every young person there had received a cross upon arrival. Francis then, in a strong voice, said: "Jesus asks, 'Do you want to help me carry the cross?'" To that question, the crowd enthusiastically responded: "We are the youth of the pope."

The language of the one percent:

Pope Benedict reminded the bishops that the theme of Vatican II was to have a "change of attitude, to one of openness and adaptation to the modern world." Despite the obvious crisis of faith that the one percent is facing, he then said: "Openness and adaptation have always characterized the authentic attitude, which shapes the approach and actions of the Church."

Who else but the one percent, whose members are living in denial, could possibly believe that they have been using their power and control in a spirit of "openness and adaptation." But I do totally agree with his assertion:

"To the extent that when this attitude is restrained or impeded, the church deteriorates rapidly."

With their tinted glasses on they can't see that that is exactly what is happening and, again in denial, he said, "Fear is often the motivating force behind such restraint and impediment." It is precisely such fear that is preventing the one percent from being "open and adapting" because they are unfamiliar with the language of the heart, which is love, which, in turn, removes fear.

And, as Hans Kung said, "It is a tragedy."

Admittedly, I have my personal biases when it comes to Pope Benedict. In any search engine, if you type in "gay marriage a threat to humanity's future: pope" you can read an entire article reported by Philip Pullella in which Benedict says gay marriage is one of several threats to the traditional family that undermine the future of humanity itself.

That statement was reaffirmed by Pope Francis, who also reaffirmed Pope Benedict's reference to the dictatorship of relativism by saying that we are to work to build peace, but there is no peace without truth and there is no truth "if everyone is out for themselves."

This stance reaffirmed the absolute and moral truth of the one percent as opposed to the ethical relativism of the masses.

Pope Francis is motivated by the courage of St. Francis to "go and build my church"—a church that he sees as "the holy people of God."

I'm sure that he realizes that other religions, those of other non-Catholic Christian communities, and those of other spiritual beliefs also see themselves among the holy people of God.

He sees the church as a "universal church," struggling with secularization, social media, and cults. Interestingly, many outside his church see his strong devotion to Mary as one such cult.

He sees the "universal church" as one charged with a moral guidance that must take seriously the plurality of social and cultural expressions affecting the church around the world. He makes it clear, and it will become clearer, that his enablers, his priests, are among the men "that God wants and, thus, do not have a private life and … live their life when they give it."

At the 2013 Holy Thursday audience with his priests, he reminded them that they were ordained to serve and they need to go out where there is need and to give anointing to those who have nothing. He reminded them that they are intermediaries, which, as a group, I refer to as a subculture. They are pastors among the sheep (those creatures on all fours), fishers of men (forget inclusive language, ladies), and they are not to be collectors of antiques. He should take a look around the museum he lives in if he wants to see who is collecting antiques.

And he most certainly hasn't forgotten about his ninety-nine percent … his sheep! He says they are in need of a profound "change of mentality."

At the 2012 Synod, the role of the laity in the new evangelization is the transmission of the "Christian Faith." Once again, I think he is referring to the Catholic Faith only.

This new evangelization will offer pastoral programs aimed at youth and families to nourish the faith and encourage conversions. Christ died for all and he urges us to evangelize, and there is no condemnation for those in the Lord Jesus. To that, all non-Catholic Christian say, "Amen!"

He has the support of those who also have concern for the environment, and for those who suffer religious persecution and threats to basic rights—with the exclusion, it would seem, of gay rights as human rights.

He says "We walk the truth," but I believe that others not of his flock do also walk the truth. He says the cross separates those who believe from those who don't, and to that I would say the cross separates those who believe in the Christian religion from those who are not Christian.

He says not to try to eliminate God and that the role of religion is essential to having a link with God, to which I would say that religion most certainly does help one in his or her relationship with God. But you can have a very spiritual life outside of a religious community, and have a deep personal relationship with the God of your understanding.

I don't believe that today's society is trying to eliminate God but rather that it is trying to find him outside of any religious community. And when he says, "Correct the worldly to return to Christ," it sounds like zealous Jesuit fervour, which did not work out so well when it was universally applied to aboriginal people.

This universal church, specifically within the one percent, believes that to be a faithful follower all you have to do is let one of those men in a pointed hat look you in the face and obey him as he says to you, "Agree with me!" But many of the enablers of the men in pointed hats, and their victims, are strong enough to have the faith, strength, and courage to say instead, "Enough!" And move beyond reconciliation!

Reflections upon Francis's talks during WYD 2013:

The Roman Catholic Institution, because of its addiction to power and control, is caught in self-absorption and self-centredness. It's not that the church is too weak; it's that the one percent has acted too strongly in always speaking against relativism, consumerism and other "isms."

Those in an addiction to power and control are distant from those they try to control, unable to respond to their needs and unable to connect by showing they care and, therefore, they lose credibility. By being caught up with itself, making itself the centre, the one percent has become merely functional, always saying, "Do as I say." It is quickly becoming a mere non-governmental organization.

It now finds itself a prisoner of its own rigid formulas, dogmas, regulations, decrees, condemnations, excommunications, and silencing of those who dared question or suggest differently.

It's not that the world has made the church a relic of the past. Rather, it's that the one percent has shown itself to be a relic of the past, unfit for new questions, as Hans Kung might say.

The one percent could speak to, or rather, it was able to order the ninety-nine percent around when it was in its infancy, when people were innocent, uneducated, easily manipulated, controlled and threatened, but not now! People have "come of age," matured, developed their own consciences, demand to be treated as equals with full inclusivity, and are aware of the language of abuse.

Today's people of the ninety-nine percent are not afraid of "going into their night" but the one percent will be very afraid of walking into a room filled with women who are not asking for but demanding equality. And using the ancient argument that Jesus was a male and a celibate won't be acceptable.

Let the one percent walk into another room filled with the thousands of gay men who were thrown out of the priesthood, not because they were pedophiles, but because of their orientation. The one percent is incapable of meeting and dialoguing with these men in the rooms in which they have been isolated by the one percent.

It's the one percent who is "wandering aimlessly alone" with its disappointments. Disillusioned, not by Christianity but, rather, by its own institution, now considered barren, fruitless soil, incapable of generating meaning. It's because of their patriarchal exclusion of women, who would be able to promote opportunities and possibilities, that they will be unable to "rediscover the maternal womb of mercy" and, by losing women, the institution will become sterile.

The one percent has been unable to offer mercy to "wounded" persons who are finding understanding, forgiveness, and love in other faith communities within and outside of religious communities. The one percent has been unable to overcome the need to manipulate and infantilize, which comes naturally for abusers.

Francis calls for self-examination by the bishops—the one percent doing its own introspection. He implies there is a lack of pastoral conversion that calls them to be close, gentle, patient, and merciful. I'm sure many won't know what he's talking about because they won't see how it applies to them.

He calls for them to love poverty, both interior and exterior, through a simple and austere life. This he says to ambitious men who are referred to as the "princes" of the church, men who wear rings that are kissed, who wear medieval clothing, and who pride themselves in taking places of honour wherever they go—honours that befit their medieval titles of Your Eminence, Excellency, Your Grace, depending on rank.

He asks these men to seek, not unanimity, but true unity in the richness of diversity. I'm sure the gay community will be curious to see where that goes.

The legacy of the one percent has been transmitted through blind obedience and submission to formulas and not through "witness," which was the initial intention of the prophet Jesus.

Jesus is, and has been preparing a new harvest for those who follow him as Christians, accepting him as the Christ, especially in various non-Catholic Christian churches. Jesus has also been preparing a new harvest for those, such as me, who are called to follow "the simple message" that he taught as a prophet, a simple message that the one percent has made complicated and incomprehensible because of its intellectual language. Other Christian denominations have kept the message simple but have been judged by the one percent as being "simplistic."

Pope Francis reminds me of Pope John XXIII. When I was just starting out in my priestly studies, along with other seminarians and many priests at that time, we were all excited by Pope John calling the church to create, in the words of Pope Francis, a proactive mindset. At the time, the emphasis was on being pastoral, not just administrative. As a subculture of priests we felt capable of warming people's hearts, walking with them, dialoguing with their hopes and disappointments, mending their brokenness.

I was very fortunate to have been ordained by George Bernard Cardinal Flahiff, 1905-1989, a man who had very strong pastoral qualities. Flahiff was one of the Council of Fathers at Vatican II and played a key role in the writing of several Conciliar documents. He was part of a great moment in church history.

Cardinal Flahiff invited the people of his time to proclaim God's truth of justice and charity in season and out of season. His interventions at the world synods of bishops in 1967 and 1971 reminded the church of our Gospel commitment to compassion, justice, equality and integrity for all people. Unfortunately, after his death we have had a succession of administrators who have had very different styles of leadership.

In response to the questions, "What has happened to the Mass?" a movement has emerged to reintroduce an "extraordinary form" of the Roman Rite, which is a phrase used in Pope Benedict XVl's motu proprio Summorum Pontificum to describe the liturgy of the 1962 Roman

Missal. Some parents say their children would love the Mass more if they were exposed to the beauty of the "extraordinary form." But when exposed, many young people only see men dressed in funny cloths who seem to belong to a different era in history ... and they do!

Those trying to promote this form say that many are not comfortable with it because it has been tied to opposition to the Second Vatican Council, which it is. The movement is trying to disentangle this belief and feels that if they are able to do so, more Catholics will feel more comfortable attending the "extraordinary form."

The cardinal of New York City added his opinion to that of many priests as "being in the agenda" of Vatican 11, which he sees as having liturgies that are "over dazzling and not realistic."

At a Mass with the clergy, Francis reminded them that they have a divine calling because Jesus said, "I have called you." These men, who are "weary and overburdened," aging and fewer in number, Francis is now calling to promote a "culture of encounter and solidarity" to make our community human. He asks them to have courage to "go against the tide." Those of us who have tried were quickly put back into our place.

He asked them to be "obsessive" in this culture of joy of encounter, with Mary as their model. The word "obsessive" comes easy to those who have an obsession to power and control.

In the last fifty years, the Catholic Church has lost at least two generations of followers, and with them, the language with which they would be able to speak with and use to evangelize the youth. How is the mass of today's youth to understand being told that the one percent has commissioned them to be instruments of the Gospel among their own families and friends, and not to fear persecution and rejection?

Rejection is exactly what the youth fear the most and the word persecution hasn't been a part of their culture. They are still learning survival skills, still having their minds educated to be conscious of themselves and their world. To ask them to "just accept" the truths, traditions, and rituals of another era and to form a community of faith with Mary as their model, and receive the Eucharist as their spiritual food, is extremely naïve.

It's too late for the one percent to find "a language" that will revive a sense of wonder at the beauty of its roots in catechesis, sacraments, Mary and the apostles. Other Christian denominations have, in the last fifty years, revived a sense of wonder in the Scriptures, community and friendship with the Lord.

When Francis asks, "What hope can we have for our present and future journey?" I say you're fifty years too late!

PART 3

Moving Beyond Reconciliation

Within Ourselves: Acceptance

*W*e had already loaded up our plates at the salad bar and buffet and starting our meal.

"Between the two of us, you were the bravest Danielle."

"How do you see that?"

"You made the decision to leave your relationship … I had to be thrown out."

"But in your book you say that you don't have any regrets … you no longer feel that way?"

"I absolutely do … otherwise I would never be able to write about our chats together, which I am furiously doing, by the way. You have validated my experience as having been an abusive one, though many will not see it that way."

"Does that concern you … that many people won't agree with you?"

"No, not really … since I can only share my experience, but doing it using the language of abuse, which both of us have been able to relate to, has validated that experience as having been abusive … I enabled it to continue for the sake of what I had perceived as my own safety and security. But what a price I paid for those things."

"Yet, just as others do when caught in an abusive relationship, I wonder if it could have worked out differently for you, Ray?"

"No, I doubt it … I was born a gay person, and because of my promiscuous lifestyle and my human need for sexual affection, it was inevitable … that in God's time I'd be forced to move on."

"What do you mean by God's time?"

"I truly believe that having been a gay male in the 60s my choices were either suicide or the priesthood. I believe that God called me to be a priest because I was gay and, thereby to be caring, creative, and sensitive to others. I was and am a kind and caring person and I know that I was a good priest who helped a lot of people go through very important and sometimes difficult times in their lives. Many men continue to be gay priests, offering these same gifts to many people. Some have secret significant others; some have become asexual, while others just haven't been caught yet. I believe that our God-given nature as sexual beings is at the heart of the issue for both lay persons and priests."

"Do you see a solution to all of this, Ray?"

"Impossible! And thanks to you, Danielle, I'm even more convinced of that."

"Thanks to me?"

"Yes, you … and our last few months of sharing are what I want to discuss with you today. What we have been through, I call a transition, and the process of getting through any transition in a healthy way involves using three specific resources, whether you're dealing with the loss of a loved one through separation or death, career changes, lifestyle changes, or retirement. These resources were initially introduced by the prophet Jesus … but I've re-worded them in today's spiritual language in my story."

Smiling slightly, Danielle replied, "Fortunately, I read your first book so I know where you're going with this, and I'm anxious to hear your once-upon-a-time story."

I smiled and continued. "Okay, so enjoy your salad as I give you my general intro to our final and most important topic." I took out my notes and began.

"Once upon a time, there was an Old Testament prophet called Moses, who, after having crossed the Red Sea with his people, to make the transition from slavery to freedom …"

"Nice connection," Danielle interjected.

"After having crossed the Red Sea with his people, Moses climbed a mountain to pray to God for guidance. In the political and religious language of the time, God spoke of obedience in recording his Ten Commandments. In the meantime, Moses was up there for so long that his people thought he must have died so they began to party and celebrate their freedom from slavery. The Book of Exodus in the Sacred Scriptures describes what happened next, which, centuries later, made for a great Hollywood movie."

"Ahhh … and it was one of the great Hollywood movies … few and far between."

"I agree, Danielle," I said as I went on. "In the New Testament of the Sacred Scriptures, we are told of the spiritual journey of another Jewish man, only thirty years old, who, after having pondered a career change to become a public speaker like his cousin, John the Baptizer, was speaking a language of a change of heart, of love and forgiveness. This was not the language of the Ten Commandments and, to stress the fact, he was cornered by a Pharisee and asked, 'According to you, Jesus, which is the greatest of the Ten Commandments?' And Jesus replied, 'The greatest Commandment is to Love God with all your heart, mind and soul, and the second is similar and just as important: Love your neighbor as yourself.'

"Jesus also said that upon those two commandments, the ten are included. In other words, the language of love was to be the central theme of all his preaching in guiding anyone who would listen to him, in making a transition from a lack of respect of others to one of love, tolerance and forgiveness.

"Many, many years later, I was asked to prepare an in-service for the staff of the two intensive care units at the hospital where I was taking pastoral-care training."

"In the footsteps of Moses, and Jesus himself ... Impressive!" Danielle said in a slightly sarcastic tone,

"As I was about to say," I said, smiling back at her. "The in-service was to help the employees make the transition from the stress of their work to finding balance and integration in their lives. So, I took Jesus' commandments and reversed them, and then referred to them as the three resources that each of us has to help us make any transition in our lives. In the language of spiritual writers of today, we make a conscious effort daily to *accept ourselves, respect others,* and *be grateful to God,* whatever, or however we understand him to be."

"Wellll," Danielle replied, dragging out the word as she said, "I may have a lot of questions about that, Ray."

"Okay, but one point at a time, Danielle," I said. "I'm already realizing that we're never going to get this covered thoroughly enough in one session."

"I agree," Danielle said with a grin. "In fact, the second you started talking about Moses, I knew we were never going to get the topic covered."

"Well, with these three resources we can live healthy, balanced lives," I said. "How I came to this awareness myself is in my book, *No Longer Lonely.*"

"And as you know, I've already read it," Danielle added, "otherwise we wouldn't be sitting here."

"And with those three resources, we can all live much happier ever after ... end of story," I said. "Look at us. We both survived years of intense experiences, which required additional years of support from family, friends, counselors and support groups. But for me, the most important support or resource was our relationship to a Higher Power, of that I'm convinced."

"I can't believe I remained a Catholic through all of that," she added, "and that you didn't ... and yet you say you continue to believe in God. It's hard for me to wrap my head around that. Nothing personal, but my mother thinks you've lost your soul."

After an explosion of laughter, I said, "Your mother isn't the only one, I'm sure. For many, it's a real struggle to say, 'I'm a Catholic, perhaps not in a state of grace, and not in good standing, but I feel that I'm a Catholic and I'll die as one.' Many feel held to the institution, and yet their faith isn't integrated into their everyday lives as it is in the cultures of some countries. Many are left with a sense of personal inadequacy, and poor self-image because they feel guilt from the insecurity, from having drifted away, from past abuse by the institutional church, from Catholic indoctrination and religious practices."

"Are you surprised anyone is left in the church, Ray, because from what you're saying, that wouldn't surprise me?"

"Not at all, Danielle. Many Catholics have a great love of the church, but many among them, including me; have difficulty with the one percent, those who govern it. You loved your family, Danielle, even Doug's mother and sisters. It was the one percent within that context … your husband … that was the issue. He was the abusive one … and the irony, if that's the right word, is that he didn't even see himself as abusive, just like the one percent! Had you confronted him, he would have denied it and been very defensive and offended. It's a parallel to the relationship I had with the church, except my one percent involved more than one person.

"The ninety-nine percent, who make up the laity and religious communities, cherish the rituals and religious traditions of their faith and the spirituality that they have been taught, to lead them to peace with God in this world and the next. I totally get that, and respect everyone who continues to cherish their faith. It's just that for me, as a gay man, I don't fit in, I am not and was not accepted by the one percent. But they didn't have anything to do with my relationship with my God."

"I see … most in my family don't attend church and don't even believe in most of the things it teaches, but speak against the church and watch out," Danielle said.

"That's because most of them fear that if the church is perceived to be wrong, then they have nothing to grasp onto when they need help since, for many, the church and God are one and the same. Many have not continued a personal relationship with their God and have not separated the one percent from the ninety-nine percent.

"In terms of the first resource, accepting myself, what I found most difficult when I was with the family," Danielle said, "was how busy I found myself, constantly running around for everyone else. And then when I sat down to read or tried to go for a walk, how guilty I felt about wasting time, or being concerned that others would perceive me as not knowing what to do with myself. I was taught to think of others first, and that thinking about myself and wanting to do something for myself was somehow being proud and selfish."

She paused to think a moment, then continued. "It sure is difficult getting rid of guilt, especially if you attach it to being a sin, and needing to be confessed to someone like yourself."

I smiled and said, "I'm assuming you're referring to when I was your parish priest."

"It's like saying to someone who is overweight that they should walk more for their health, or to a smoker that the habit will bring on other complications, or to a someone addicted to so-called reality shows that reading might be more brain stimulating. It's often taken badly and they want to tell you, if they don't actually tell you, to please mind your own business, or they sarcastically say, 'Look who's calling the kettle black.' It feels like talking to a wall."

"No one is ready for any of that advice unless they want to hear it or they're ready to hear it," I said. "And that is an essential point in the spirituality of writers such as Dyer, Tolle, Louise Hay, and so many others, that unless you're willing to make a conscious decision to grow, growth won't happen. As they put it: 'We have entered a new era in our human evolution,' and refer to it as 'a time of conscious awareness and awakening.'

"It's usually at that time when we reach bottom," I went on, "or when we're looking for, or praying for support that God or the Universe synchronistically allows us to meet a spiritual messenger or to read or hear the words of wisdom we need. I believe such events and words come to anyone on any religion or spiritual path who is open to faith and trust, which are essential to accepting yourself ... that first resource."

"But," Danielle said, "We are confronted with so many conflicting messages about how we should look, what we should eat, and what we should do. Where do you start?"

"As some wise person once said, and don't ask me who, you just take one step at a time. Each one of us has a powerful survival tool that is ingrained within us. Unfortunately, many of us don't trust it enough and others ignore it totally, and that's our gut instinct. If I feel good about doing something and you don't, you could be influenced by me, but you're blessed with the instinct not to go along with what I'm saying. For whatever reason, God is trying to tell you not to go along. What may be acceptable to me may not be acceptable to you and that requires respect and reverence and gratitude to a Higher Power for guiding and protecting us."

"Ray, how do we help with the first step?"

"We have all inherited what I call survival tools or resources that are ingrained in us naturally, or put there at an early age by our parents or guardians, and later by others who come into our lives and whom we learn from. Most of our guardians taught us what to believe and gave us values that were important to being accepted within the family unit, within school and society. Not bullying should have been emphasized more, as we're realizing today.

In my PowerPoint presentations, I say that we can nourish our minds through studying and learning, which give us a capacity to process ideas, to be able to organize our thoughts, giving us an openness and a vocabulary, an alertness. Improving our memory through reading, we are given a language with which to express our own experiences and a challenge to respect and understand different points of view. "Through the Arts, we are opened to a world of creativity, imagination, wonder, thought, emotions and beauty."

Danielle chuckled and said, "Somehow I didn't see all that in studying Math and English, let alone the school concerts. Did you?"

"Not quite, the problem is that we are trained to do things and don't understand why we are doing them or the benefits and skills they provide us. But you have to remember that those who were teaching us often didn't know any of this either, and trying to convince us at the time wouldn't have sounded very convincing. We needed more years of maturing and personal experience to put the skills and lessons together to provide us with a powerful resource ... Some learn and others don't, and life moves on."

"Ray, you mentioned the body ... I think our society is doing quite a job on that one, don't you, in terms of accepting ourselves?"

"It's doing quite a job all right, to the point of obsession ... The ways we can care for or nourish our bodies, as we are all aware, are through exercise, sufficient sleep and eating well. Though we are often preoccupied with our body image, we shouldn't neglect to nourish our minds and spirit as well ... in order to have balance within ourselves. There is more to us than our bodies."

"When you speak of spirit, what are you referring to?"

"So far, I've been able to rim off a Webster dictionary definition I like, 'intellectual or moral state; - often in the plural; as, to be cheerful, or in good spirits; to be downhearted, or in bad spirits.[4]' We can care for or nourish our spirit through nature, which fosters respect, wonder, serenity, solitude, and a yearning and appreciation of beauty. Through meditation, we foster love, and a sense of meaning and purpose. Through music, we foster wonder, and emotions. And through rest we foster self-care and love. These are all ways of caring for our spirit. You've heard the expression that someone has gotten out on the wrong side of the bed, which generally means they are in a bad mood?"

---

[4]   See for example: www.definitions.net/definition/spirit

"Unfortunately, yes, I can recall being asked a few times which side of the bed I had gotten up from," Danielle replied.

"It's all part of the conscious awareness that spiritual writers are talking about today. For example, as soon as we awake we have a choice we can make, and it does take a conscious decision on our part. We can either pound the alarm clock off, full of resentment, and exclaim, 'Oh my God, another day!' or we can wake up saying, 'Oh Thank you God, another day.' The decision is ours, and it takes a conscious decision to greet the day with gratitude and with a positive spirit. Whichever we choose decides the energy that we will attract to ourselves from those we encounter in the hours that follow, and the events that will unfold. Having a balance or harmony within ourselves, between our mind, body, and spirit, requires an acceptance of ourselves, and we are responsible for our choices."

"Sounds like work, Ray. I definitely see that it takes a conscious decision … and I have to admit that when I get up I'm still dazed, and to thank God for the new day at that moment would take some conscious effort, for sure!"

"Try it Danielle, and let me know how it makes you feel, and how the day then unfolds."

"Sounds as if we're going to be meeting again," she said.

"You're not surprised are you, Danielle?"

"I know that when I speak to my mother about this conscious awareness spirituality she is going to wonder if I'm preparing to leave the church."

"Not at all Danielle! This is meant for everyone, of all religions and for those of us outside of formal religions. As I mentioned earlier, we have entered a new era in our human evolution ... a time of conscious awareness and awakening.

An awakening that makes us more aware of how we are living in the present moment, which Eckhart Tolle speaks so well about in his books *The Power of Now* and *A New Earth*.

"I think I get it, Ray ... It's just so unfortunate that so many of us feel so guilty about taking care of ourselves."

"Taking care of ourselves, Danielle, is to honor ourselves, which builds self-esteem and releases negative energy. So the most important word to remember as we try to maintain a balance within ourselves between our mind, body and spirit is 'acceptance.'"

"And with that," I continued, "I think we are now ready to talk about our second resource ... respect for others and our relationships with them."

With some alarm in her voice, Danielle promptly replied, "Surely we aren't going to tackle that one today!"
"No, no," I said. "I think it would make a good start to our next chat ... In the meantime, how are you feeling about all this Danielle?"

"Well, let me put it this way ... I'm sure that being aware of all this could have helped me a lot when I was an enabler, but it will help me to stay more positive and grateful into the future."

"That's what it's all about Danielle. Being able to accept ourselves, even as enablers, and know that we are not alone. That's what we'll talk about next time."

Between Ourselves: Respect

*J*wo weeks later, as Danielle approached my table at the Paddlewheel, I got right into it. "Hi Danielle ... Ready to talk about your in-laws?"

She laughed as she sat down with her lunch and said, "Yes Ray ... And I'm also ready to look into your subculture, as you refer to the priesthood."

"Great! Let's start by thinking about the second resource, respect for others, those with whom we are in a relationship. They can include family, significant others, children, relatives, and all those in our work, leisure, social life, religious groups, and support groups. These connections can offer us friendships and hospitality, and can teach us about involvement, co-operation and adaptability. They can also help us when we need to adjust to change and when we need someone to listen to us. And, of course, they offer us the opportunity to appreciate differences ... Now how's that for a mouthful to start lunch ... no pun intended."

"Almost as good as this salad ... and if I may, shall we chew on it awhile?"

I laughed as I dived into my own lunch and Danielle responded to what I had been saying.

"It all sounds great, Ray, but in the midst of those relationships, I didn't think about what they were offering me or what I could be getting out of them. But I do admit that Doug's in-laws were very kind and welcoming to me, and I did like them. Many in the church and community were very kind and I enjoyed being with them. I know that I could have asked to speak to many of them but I was afraid of what might happen if anyone lacked discretion and gossiped. My life would have been a living hell and I would have felt all alone. Thank goodness we had an unlimited long-distance phone plan and, since I was the one paying the bills, he didn't see all the weekly calls I was making to my mother and friends. If his mother had disliked him I would have had a strong ally, but she adored him ... go figure!"

"Relationships can often be painful when we are dealing with the guilt and regrets of the past, or with concerns about the future, and not knowing how to live in the reality of the present."

"I find that's especially true when you leave a relationship," she replied. "When you meet people later that you knew during the relationship, they seem awkward ... and don't seem to know what to say. I find myself being the ice-breaker."

"That's been my experience also Danielle, once a person steps outside of the norms of a family unit, no one knows how to react or what to say to them. There are priests I have known for twenty years but when we meet now, they look stunned and don't know what to say to me. On the one hand, they might feel that I have abandoned ship, and on the other hand, they are happy for me once they know that I'm okay. Many of us have lived within the expectations of others. To live our own lives takes courage, support and faith."

"Letting go of the relationship is one thing," Danielle said, easily adding to the flow of the conversation. "And then you deal with the guilt of starting a new relationship, and all the church regulations around that, especially if you don't want an annulment and you don't want to get married in the church. Now you have your own family concerned about your soul and sexual life. The pressure from within and outside can be overwhelming at times."

"I know what you're saying, Danielle, because moving on often requires tremendous courage and strength, especially since many of the decisions you will be making will not be supported by family, or even your own friends. This second resource, by definition, involves others in our life, and often changes greatly during a time of transition, but the resources are there if we have said enough, and if we have God guiding us as we move on.

"Having support from family and friends," I went on, "makes talking about your experience easier. If they are not supportive, then you find a counsellor and support groups that are made up of individuals like you who are going through similar situations. There are such groups for every transition known to our human experiences. It takes some searching, but they exist and sometimes we have to travel a distance to connect, but when you find them, everyone in the group will understand with empathy what you're going through."

"Letting go of our guilt is so difficult. Why is that, Ray?"

"Let me try to explain through my own experience. When I was a child, I believed what my parents taught us about our faith and its practices. Why would I question them? They were handing down to me what they believed and hoped that it would help me in my life. As a priest, I preached what I believed and had been taught.

For example, you must go to church on Sundays or you're committing a mortal sin, and you need to confess it to a priest, of course. I'm sure I made many people feel guilty if they missed Mass on Sunday and if they didn't confess their sin."

"I must have confessed that one at least once to you," Danielle admitted with a smile.

"At the time, I believed in what I was preaching. But as time went on and my understanding grew, I began to doubt what I believed and what I was teaching. Providence helped me leave the priesthood. One would think that I'd be filled with all sorts of guilt. And I believe that had I not had support groups and counsellors through my transition while working at Headingley Corrections, I would have remained angry, judgmental, resentful and negative toward the church. I have met people who, as soon as they started talking about the Catholic Church, filled up with anger, their faces looked as if they were about to erupt."

"So many people feel they have been hurt by the church, Ray."

"And that's why I speak about the church as being ninety-nine percent the faithful and only one percent the hierarchy, whose power and control has hurt many people.

I paused to sip my coffee and Danielle asked, "How do you stop them from erupting and going on and on, ragging against the church?"

"When they start welling up, I listen to see where their anger is being directed. Is it toward a certain teaching, a particular priest, or an incident, and then I can tell them that I understand. Many feel that in leaving the church, that they have disappointed someone, or even God. Living up to others' expectations and depending on their acceptance of us is deeply ingrained in many people.

"It's difficult to simply say I understand, without adding fuel to the fire," I added. "And you can only do that when you have moved on ... beyond reconciliation. This is what we are talking about. It's impossible to do that without respecting the person's right to have a different point of view and not judge them for it, and stand up for what you believe. And it's difficult, at times, to speak up for what we believe, yet, if we don't we will feel either anger at the other person's view, or disappointment in ourselves for not having had the courage to share our point of view without self-reproach or judgment. At the same time, each time we share our point of view, without self-righteousness, we become stronger in our courage to share our faith."

"And by faith you mean?"

"What you believe in, which usually involves your relationship with a Higher Power, which I want to talk some more about later. If you get your self-worth and acceptance by agreeing with others and going along with what they want to do, you're on shaky ground, and even more so when you start having strongly different views and opinions. That's what was happening to me as a priest. But if the others can respect your view and opinions, your faith, as you respect theirs, then there can be openness and a freedom to grow. How do you live in a family that doesn't accept you as being gay and having the human right to be in a loving, gay relationship?"

"Being gay seems to be an important issue for you, Ray."

"Of course ... because I now realize that being gay, having intimate relationships with other gay men and God, and writing about the experience, sharing the experience with others, counselling others when asked, is what my spiritual journey on this planet is all about.

"Many won't agree with you, Ray, and, of course, you know that, but how do you handle it?"

"You're right Danielle. I've lost friends and relatives over my orientation and lifestyle. But I'm still the same person they knew before they knew about that part of my life. We will all know people whose circumstances in life will change and whose choices will be different from our own, and we can either reject them or respect them. It hurts when others reject us but we have no control over that, and we need to continue to respect their choice to no longer accept us. That's why mutual respect, or reverence, is required for healthy relationships to exist; otherwise we have to move beyond the possibility of reconciliation by accepting the fact that reconciliation is not possible. And be grateful for what was in order to move forward from a positive stance. I am grateful toward the Catholic Church for the great education I received, the wonderful people I met, and for the strong spiritual formation I received. As they say, we have to 'Let go and let God' so that when you do say 'enough,' it comes from an inner place of peace."

"Powerful stuff, Ray … and speaking of gratitude and appreciation, I feel quite blessed having the opportunity to share all this with you. Really, it's great, and I thank you for it." "Well, thank you Danielle, but do realize this is mutual. You are helping me along the path just as much as I may be helping you … but before we get too far into forming an official mutual admiration society, I have a story that I'd like to leave with you today."

"Oh, great! I love a good story."

"Here goes … and, by the way, I've told this story many times so I apologize if you've heard it before, maybe as one of my parishioners …

"One day, a man who could have been a Muslim, a Jew, a Hindu, or a Christian, was hiking and enjoying his inner peace so much he was distracted from the task at hand and walked right off a cliff."

"My goodness, Ray! I hope this is not too violent."

"No, no … his fall was broken by a shrub growing out of the side of the cliff. As he dangled there holding onto the shrub for his life, he did what many of us would do in a similar situation. With no one around to help him, and facing imminent death, he began to pray."

"Something tells me I should take this story with a grain of salt," Danielle said.

"Don't spoil my punch line Danielle. As I was saying, he began to pray, as any good Muslim, Jew, Hindu or

Christian would. Suddenly, he heard a voice from above saying, 'Do you believe in God?'

'Oh yes, God, you know I believe in you.'

'That's good,' came the clear and certain reply. 'Then let one hand go.'

"The man thought for a moment … and believed he could hang on with just one hand, so he let go of his grip with the other.

'Okay, I'm holding on with only one hand God,' he said, and the voice from above replied. 'Do you still believe in me?'

'Oh yes, God, I told you, I believe in you.'

'That's good,' came the response. 'Then let the other hand go as well.'

The man, eyes wide, reflected on the command from above as he looks first upward, and then below, and then skyward again as he hollered: 'Is there anyone else up there?'

As we both laughed, Danielle said, "That wasn't bad at all, Ray. Do you have other stories like that?"

"Yes, I do … Remember, I was a priest for a long time, and I certainly know how our faith is often put to the test, which is what I would like to explore next time we meet … starting with a blessing before we eat."

"A blessing?" Danielle replied with surprise. "After all these months we have never said a single blessing before we ate."

"I know Danielle, and I feel guilty about that, so I decided to start … next time."

"Forgive me for being suspicious, Ray, but I have to say, I am intrigued … and looking forward to it."

With Our Higher Power: Gratitude

*W*hen we met again, Danielle looked like she was in a prayerful mood, or perhaps it was just me looking forward to getting into the topic of prayer with her.

We went through our usual greetings and foraging routine at the buffet before we sat down.

"So Ray," she began in a sarcastic tone. "I couldn't wait to get my meal over here and have you pray over it."

"Sorry to disappoint you Danielle," I replied, "but I'm going to start by talking about praying without actually doing it. Though I'm always grateful for what we have to share."

"Okay, if it's not actual prayer we're doing today, I'm guessing the topic is our relationship with God, correct?"

"That's it Danielle, the third resource, God and gratitude. As I said a couple of weeks ago, I have another story to share with you. So I'll let you savor your gourmet salad as I begin."

"Someone else falling over a cliff?" she asked.

"No," I said with a chuckle. "Although this one also has a man walking through the woods ... He too is enjoying the moment when he hears some loud cracking and brushing of twigs behind him. He turns around to see a large grizzly bear standing on its hind legs and coming toward him ... So what do you suppose he does in such a situation?"

"Let me guess; would prayer be the right answer?"

"Good guess Danielle. So, this guy closes his eyes and begs God to make this grizzly a Christian bear. Suddenly, there is stillness ... and he remains standing."

"God zapped the bear and everyone lived happily ever after?"

"Not quite. The man opens his eyes to see the bear kneeling with its front paws together and its head down, seemingly in prayer."

"This better have a good ending."

"So, of course the man is curious as to what the bear could possibly be saying."

"Understandably."

"So he walks cautiously up to the bear to better hear its words of prayer: 'Bless me, oh Lord, for the food I'm about to receive."

With a roar of laughter from Danielle, and a more restrained version from me, she said, "Not bad Ray ... and the lesson is to be careful about what you pray for."

"Exactly!"

After giving our lunches their due attention for a few minutes, Danielle reignited the conversation. "Now that you're no longer in the priesthood, and the church, may I ask if you still pray, Ray?"

"Every day, all day long," I said. "As you know, as Catholics we had many ways of praying, many of which you probably still practice. I know my sisters still do. There's the Mass, prayers of devotion to the saints and, of course, to the Blessed Virgin Mary, especially with the rosary. And I used to encourage people just to talk to God from their hearts. Most of the praying was asking for something. For example, if I was sick, I'd pray to get well."

"And now you don't pray to get well anymore?"

"Now, if I am sick, I thank God for helping me get better. My prayer, or intention as I often refer to it, is now about thanking God for assisting me in my present situation."

"What if God takes a week or more to answer?" she asked.

"Well, I have a story about a man who was walking in the woods and suddenly falls off a cliff."

"You never did say what happened to that guy dangling there on that branch."

Ignoring the question, except for a slight smile, I asked Danielle if she had prayed when she was going through her difficult relationship.

"I prayed the rosary every day … thanks, in part, to my mother's constant insistence. And, yes, it helped. We went as a family to Sunday Mass, surrounded by his family and our friends … only God and I knowing what was going on … and the children. I'm not too sure what my husband was praying for. Peace on earth perhaps."

"We need another prophet like Jesus to awaken humanity to live a balanced life in a spirit of humble gratitude. We have an entire generation that feels that it has a 'right of entitlement' and they want the best of everything and they want it now. They are very competitive and driven by consumerism and materialism. And their parents, who abandoned a personal relationship with God, were not able to pass this resource or spiritual relationship on to their children, so it is foreign to them today. I sometimes hear of a spiritual revival in the works in the near future and I hope so because something needs to happen to awaken us spiritually."

"I know that when the topic of God comes up, whether it's through climatic or world events, it sure can create some strong reactions and opinions," Danielle said.

"Jesus gave us the formula, and the three essential resources, now I feel we need to learn how to relate in a positive way to our Higher Power for a healthy, balanced life. As I've mentioned, some relate to a Higher Power in support groups, whether religious or not, in nature, retreats, yoga, Tai chi, or meditation. And this relationship to God develops serenity, joy, wonder, solitude, a sense of meaning, purpose, gratitude, and self-esteem. All creativity comes from stillness, which is difficult for many people today. Fortunately, many indigenous cultures are rediscovering their native rituals and cultures."

Once again, our time together had come to an end. We sat in quietly for a few minutes finishing our coffee, and then Danielle broke the silence as she rose from her chair.

"Well, Ray, as a Christian, I show my acceptance and agreement with everything we have shared, and I say Amen, and leave you with gratitude."

"Thank you Danielle," I replied. "It has truly been a pleasure and a wonderful journey ... and I'm sure we will stay in touch."

"Namaste, Danielle."

"Namaste, Ray."

A Reflection

*T*he arts, and my human experiences, have taught me in a way that has been captivating and memorable. I enjoy visual stimulation and learning through seeing. I believe our brains, when taking in new visual stimuli, often improve the learning for many of us.

The movie *Philomena* was one such visual learning experience for me. It is the true story of a mother's search for her lost son, based on the celebrated book by Martin Sixsmith, *The Lost Child of Philomena Lee*, published in 2009. The movie serves as an excellent visual example of what I refer to as "moving beyond reconciliation."

When she got pregnant as a teenager in Ireland in 1950s, Philomena was sent to the convent of Roscrea to be looked after. She was what the Catholic hierarchy (the one percent) would call a "fallen women" (pregnant and unwed). That meant the nuns would serve as enablers by selling the newborn children for adoption in America. The nuns' actions were blessed by the Catholic Institution because the mothers were seen as having been sinful, and if they were seen that way by the church, they would be seen that way by God also.

Philomena spent the next fifty years searching in vain for her son. Then she met Martin Sixsmith, a world-weary political journalist who happened to be intrigued by her story. Critics call the film a compelling narrative of human love and loss, and ultimately a celebration of life—true enough, but I see it as much more than that. For me, Philomena is a perfect example of someone who moved beyond reconciliation, but Martin was not able to go that far.

Despite all the denials and the lies from the nuns and the years of anguish they had caused Philomena, she is able to say, "Enough!" and walks out of the church. She has realized that the nuns did what they had felt was right, and being angry at them would only fill her with resentment and bitterness and not bring her son back to her. She was moving beyond reconciliation, which was impossible.

Not all nuns were created equal, of course. One day, a young nun gives Philomena a photo of her son, which she had stolen from the files. She would have been seriously disciplined for that, and might have been, since she was later transferred from that convent.

Towards the end of the movie, Philomena and Martin confront the aged nun who had played a big part in parting her from her son. The nun looks at Philomena with the same distain and self-righteousness that filled her when they were much younger. Philomena looks at her and says, "I just want you to know that I forgive you." The aged nun, still filled with the same denial and venom, responds that she has nothing to be forgiven for and that she has only

God to answer to, since she was only doing the will of the church, and hence of God.

Books, movies, and the popular media's exposure of the injustices of the Catholic Institution has served as a catalyst for thousands of adopted Irish children and their "shamed" mothers to come forward; for thousands of sexually abused children by pedophile priests in residential schools and parishes; for thousands of gay priests being used as scapegoats for the homophobic one percent, which denies the right of their own gay clergy to "own their truth;" and for the thousands of victims of inquisitions, excommunications, and financial embezzlements and laundering.

The one percent is quick to remind us of all the great charities and services they provide, which they generously do, but the bad seems to overshadow any humble good gestures.

It is only when we are able to say "Enough!" that we are prepared to transition emotionally, physically and spiritually.

A Parable

After forty years of marriage, Martha finds herself alone in the village home in which she and her husband raised their four children. In this village everyone is known by name. The pain of her loss is always in her heart and memories.

She rises early and prepares herself for another day of repeated rituals, washing up, prayers, breakfast, and a stroll through her garden and flower beds. Neighbours pass by and chat, a friend might drop in for tea, and the mailman might have a delivery.

But today will be different, in fact, special, but with a certain apprehension. The church minister is dropping in for his yearly census, just in case either of them have news to offer the other. He's new to the community and, therefore, filled with good intentions and enthusiasm.

"Good morning Mrs. Irving," he says as he enters the widow's home.

"Please, Father, call me Martha ... and yes, it is a good morning, and so nice having you visit. Please come in Father."

As he enters her home, he is overcome by the colours of all the flowering African violets on almost every flat surface, window ledge, small table, cabinet, and as table centrepieces. They are an easy conversation starter and an obvious point of interest for both of them.

"Martha, I've never seen such beautiful plants ... Your love for each other is obvious."

"Thanks Father ... I started them while my husband was still alive and their presence continues to keep me company."

"Have you sold them at parish sales?" he asks.

"Ohh, no Father, I don't want to make money from them, but I do offer them to everyone who visits, including first-time visitors," she says as she smiles at him.

"I didn't know if I dare ask, but I hope that's an offer you're making Martha?"

The pleasant conversation continued for some time over tea and, of course, fresh cookies. Finally, the minister, with his new gift in hand, left Martha's house anxious to speak to his parish council about an idea that occurred to him while sipping tea. He wanted the support of the council to ask Martha if she would be willing to offer one of her plants, on behalf of the parish community, to every new parishioner and newlywed in the parish, at baptisms, and at funerals. The parish would supply planters, paper and wrappings, and whatever else she needed to offer the plants as special gifts on behalf of the parish. Council sent a representative to speak to Martha to make the arrangements and discuss any concerns she might have, and soon the idea went forward.

As the years went by, Father and Martha both grew in recognition and gratitude. Martha's daily rituals remained as usual, except for the occasional special offering being prepared. She would often get messages of gratitude from those who had received a "parish gift" thanks to her.

One day, the minister got a call that he found so difficult to receive. "I am sorry Father," the caller told him, "but Martha has passed away."

"Father, what are we going to do?" asked a concerned member of the parish council. "The whole town wants to attend the funeral, and we've been getting calls from outside the parish. We won't be able to fit more than our usual parish community into the church."

On the day of the funeral, Martha's children were confused as to why the funeral wasn't being held in the church that their mother had loved so much for so many years. The minister, on hearing of their concern, quickly gathered them together and told them that they would understand once they got into the community hall.

As they entered, they were overtaken by emotion. It was filled to capacity.

One of her children said "Father, I don't understand why all these people are here. Mom was a simple home keeper who lived her life quietly. Who are all these people? I don't understand why they would all want to be here."

After a tearful explanation, another of her children asked about the significance of that very large plant at the base of her casket.

"Your Mom gave me that plant eight years ago," Father said, "and I wanted her to smile upon it today."

God has given each of us natural gifts, talents to be used not only for ourselves but also to be shared with others and, thereby, give thanks to the God of our understanding for the ability to love and be loved.

Printed in the United States
By Bookmasters